AFRICAN AMERICAN
PASTORAL CARE
AND COUNSELING

AFRICAN AMERICAN PASTORAL CARE AND COUNSELING

THE POLITICS OF OPPRESSION AND EMPOWERMENT

EDWARD P. WIMBERLY

THE
PILGRIM
PRESS
Cleveland

To Walter G. Muelder, 1907–2004,
who gave direction to Boston University School of Theology over many years.
He assembled a wonderful faculty that included professors of Social
Ethics/Sociology of Religion and Pastoral Psychology and Counseling.
It was the Boston University School of Theology environment that shaped my
academic interest in linking pastoral psychology and counseling
with social, cultural, and political concerns.

The Pilgrim Press
700 Prospect Avenue
Cleveland, Ohio 44115-1100
thepilgrimpress.com

© 2006 by Edward P. Wimberly

All rights reserved. Published 2006

Printed in the United States of America on acid-free paper

10 09 08 07 06   5 4 3 2 1

Library of Congress Cataloging-in-Publication Data
Wimberly, Edward P., 1943-
    African American pastoral care and counseling : the politics
of oppression and empowerment / Edward P. Wimberly.
        p. cm.
    ISBN 0-8298-1681-X
    1. African Americans – Pastoral counseling of. 2. Church work
with African Americans.   I. Title.
BV4468.2.A34W56 1997
253.089'96073 – dc22
                                                        2005028967
ISBN-13 978-0-8298-1681-5
ISBN-10 0-8298-1681-X

Contents

Foreword

"The personal is political." I can still recall how those words hit me when I first read José Míguez Bonino's book *Christian Political Ethics*. His analysis detailed how simple, seemingly private consumer decisions by North Americans were affecting the economies of cities and villages in faraway parts of the developing world. Míguez Bonino and other Latin American liberation theologians urged Christians in the First World to be aware of the political and economic impact of their personal behavior, and, above all, to be better stewards of our resources. One part of the church pleaded with another part to act and spend in ways that could help the poor people who produced those goods, empower their villages, sustain the natural environment, and pressure governments to support human rights for all people.

When I first read this, I thought, *That's a tall order for folks who just want a good cup of coffee or scoop of ice cream.* Yet several U.S. companies began to get the message and adopt socially responsible business practices. But I also faintly recalled that Dr. King had said something similar back in the 1960s. Recall his words in *Where Do We Go from Here: Chaos or Community?*

> All people are interdependent, . . . Whether we realize it or not, each of us lives eternally "in the red." We are everlasting debtors to known and unknown men and women.

7

When we arise in the morning, we go into the bathroom where we reach for a sponge which is provided for us by a Pacific Islander. We reach for soap that is created for us by a European. Then at the table we drink coffee which is provided for us by a South American, or tea by a Chinese or cocoa by a West African. Before we leave for our jobs we are already beholden to more than half of the world.... All life is interrelated.... Whatever affects one directly affects all indirectly.[1]

Long before this insight had entered the public consciousness, Dr. King helped to focus attention on public dimensions of private life.

Now comes Ed Wimberly's important book that links politics and pastoral care, two practices I haven't seen connected very often. The notion that American religion is privatized is not a new one. Rauschenbusch, Niebuhr, and King alerted us to this long ago and suggested that we give greater emphasis to the social, political, and public dimensions of the gospel just to correct the culture's imbalance. But most of us never suspected that pastoral care would be a significant discipline in the movement to "publicize theology." Ethics, of course; theology, yes; but pastoral care? No way!

In fact, there has been a long history of pastoral theologians and psychologists who have situated their work on the mind and soul within a socio-political-cultural context. Wimberly's book stands in that tradition and comes at a critical time in the life of theological education and religious practice in America.

There is a raging debate afoot within black church culture about the appropriate balance of personal and political construal of the Christian message. The center of black church culture has always sought to maintain a fragile and elusive "middle way," illustrated in King's ministry. King was a pastor first, who preached, counseled, taught, and guided church members into a deeper encounter with the Holy. The other, non-congregation-based activities that unfolded in his public ministry were outgrowths of that fundamental pastoral identity at the center of the man.

But the "middle way" has not held. On one hand — the left — it has yielded to some liberation thinkers who rarely speak of spiritual growth, intimacy with God, healthy interpersonal relationship skills, and a good psyche. And on the right hand, it has lost ground to those who embrace the "Christ against culture" that H. R. Niebuhr set forth decades ago. They ignore or disdain politics and justice talk in the service of delivering souls to the kingdom. And, on yet another hand, there are the "prosperity preachers" of late who read the gospel as a manual for personal wealth accumulation. ("The foxes have holes and the birds have nests but the Son of Man has nowhere to lay his head." Go figure.) All of these iterations of modern faith seem errant and in need of correction. *African American Pastoral Care and Counseling* may be just what we needed at this hour in history.

Wimberly, like King, is a product of the Boston University School of Theology where the balanced approach has been prominent. But before the fancy graduate education, also like King, he lived in the home of a pastor and listened to the conversations of his parents (not just his father). In fact, as we encounter his mother in these pages, we hear the moral authority and hermeneutic of suspicion that has been the gift of black women to world Christianity. She kept Wimberly's father honest about his brand of pastoral counseling and provided for her son an example of the kind of vigorous debate about the personal/public dialectic that should animate all of our pastoral imaginations.

Wimberly is one of the nation's premier African American pastoral theologians and is at the top of his game. This book could advance a much-needed approach to a complicated conversation about the kind of pastoral care best suited for people who have known racism, sexism, poverty, and religious abuse. In light of the debate in the black church, it is providential that he teaches and administers at the Interdenominational Theological Center (ITC), the nation's largest black seminary, where he has access to current and future church leadership that can reset the agenda in this field. I've had the privilege of knowing and working with him for many years and think that his dedication, warmth, intelligence, and charisma will transform this book into a tool for opening closed minds and closing open arguments that do not liberate.

ROBERT M. FRANKLIN
Presidential Distinguished Professor of Social Ethics
Candler School of Theology, Emory University

The Politics
of African American
Pastoral Care and Counseling

It is because pastoral care and counseling facilitate personal agency and efficacy — or one could say personal, social, and political empowerment and transformation — that I contend that African American pastoral care and counseling are inherently political processes. In this book I outline a theological anthropology that undergirds the practices of care and the practices of the self as holistic processes. Yet such a theological anthropology and such practices of care critique the culture of modernity that is undermining precisely the relational institutions that support personal and political efficacy.

The book argues that the political process exists to enable individuals and groups of people to participate fully in society at every level to the extent of their gifts and capacities.[1] Racism, however, seeks to limit this participation for African Americans primarily through recruiting African Americans into negative self-images, identities, and stories. Such recruiting leads African Americans to internalize oppression, keeping them in psychic bondage without even needing overt forms of oppression to reinforce racism. The most fundamental role of pastoral counseling with this clientele is therefore to liberate African Americans from the negative images, identities, and stories into which they have been recruited, and to accompany them in discerning how best to make use of their resulting personal and political agency and efficacy.

At the heart of recruiting of African Americans into negative stories and at the heart of disenfranchisement is how scarce resources are allocated. Politics is about who has access to the vast range yet finite supply of resources needed for human fulfillment.[2] Politics is a deadly game of limiting access to scarce resources by any means necessary. It is the dominant — read white — groups who do the limiting, and because the imposed limitations typically revolve around race, a favored strategy of the white dominant group is to reinforce negative perceptions among and of other racial groups in order to both appear to legitimize the power imbalances and actually stymie healthy self-perception.

Into this vicious political and personal cycle steps pastoral counseling. It seeks first to liberate persons from internalized conversations and stories into which they have been recruited and which limit their ability to participate in wider society at all levels. Second, as a political process, pastoral counseling seeks to strengthen those mediating structures such as the nuclear family, extended family, the local congregation, and social networks that are already in place to support personal and political efficacy. Third, pastoral counseling brings to the public arena insights from the pastoral counseling process that critique social forces undermining human worth and dignity, particularly modernity. And fourth, pastoral counseling promotes practices of self, which enable individuals to be connected relationally and which in turn enables active agency on behalf of self and others.

Several key features of this book need to be spelled out at the beginning. First, most counseling is understood as promoting and extending wider cultural values and interests. Rarely is it thought of as vehicle for critical analysis and reform of society. This book provides an alternative view of pastoral care and counseling, and of counseling and therapy in general.

Second, the book also reverses the explicit individualism that undergirds much of counseling psychological thinking by instead presenting a holistic view of human beings — that they cannot be understood without their social context. Indeed, human beings cannot be whole without connecting their private lives with their public lives as well as their personal selves with their social selves.

A recent publication provides a historical sketch of the development of public theology in the United States,[3] but does so without developing in depth how public theology grows out insights generated by reflection on the pastoral counseling process itself. This book links public theology to the insights that have grown out of the pastoral counseling process itself, thus showing the holistic links inherent in pastoral counseling from the beginning.

Chapter by Chapter

Chapter 1 explores in depth African American pastoral care and counseling as political processes. It shows how contemporary approaches to pastoral care and counseling typically ignore the role of pastoral caregivers in addressing political processes. Four dimensions of pastoral care and counseling as political processes are outlined with a focus on power and its implications for pastoral care and counseling. Selected theories of Australian family therapist Michael White are drawn on to help us understand how pastoral counseling is inherently a political process.

Chapter 2 examines the original membership contexts in which I grew up that help to illustrate how I learned that pastoral counseling is a political process. Such an exploration shows how context influences us to internalize messages, conversations, and discourses that enable us as African Americans to participate fully outside our original membership communities and in other communities that help us to fulfill our lives and calling. Because individuals' communities of original memberships, such as the nuclear family, extended family, and the local congregation, help to mediate the internalization process of wider cultural images, the role of such original membership communities is to assure the internalization of positive images, messages, identities, and stories. I draw on my own experiences within my family of origin as well as in the local congregation and graduate school as illustrative material, and suggest practices of re-membership that lead to personal and political efficacy.

Chapter 3 explores how personal agency leads to political agency in the lives of several African American authors who have written their memoirs. The focus is on how pastoral care and therapeutic counseling were used to edit the original identities, stories, and scripts into which they were recruited in ways to increase their personal and political agency. E. Lynn Harris was recruited into negative feelings of self-worth by sexual abuse. We read how therapy liberated him to affirm himself as worthwhile and loved by God. The second is a story of Linda Hollies, a black minister, who was recruited into a negative identity through sexual abuse and tells how therapy and other experiences served to help her edit internalized oppression and facilitate personal and political agency. The third story is about Wilson Goode, the former mayor of Philadelphia, whose school sought to undermine his intellectual ability through teachers who were racist; it tells how counsel from church members countered the teachers' recruiting efforts.

Chapter 4 explores how the practices of self relate to connecting one's private and public lives and how such connecting is essential for contemporary clergy. This chapter shows how pastoral counseling can be used to counter societal messages that coerce us to accept a limited understanding of human nature in ways that undermine our identity. I draw on the work of novelist Ernest J. Gaines to help explore how negative wider cultural conversations are internalized by some African Americans and how such conversations can be addressed in counseling. In addition, I suggest how pastoral counselors can address the public debate about separating our private and public lives, how to adopt practices of self that lead to authentic living, and what role the development of emotional intelligence has in such practices of self.

Chapter 5 explores how life crises are impacted by cultural conversations and the role of pastoral care in sorting through conversations that have the potential of derailing the life cycle process. Often these conversations cripple personal and political efficacy. Illustrations from the novel *The Emperor of Ocean Park* by Stephen Carter suggest how pastoral care can foster personal and political efficacy during the midlife crisis, and particularly how a more nuanced understanding of modernity can open our eyes to its impact on practices of self in the United States.

Chapter 6 focuses on African American pastoral care and counseling as public theology. It defines the role of African American pastoral care and counseling as political theology that challenges how modernity has created a value system that reduces human worth and value to commodities that can be bought and sold on the open market. We see that post-modernity stresses the significance of building our identity on spiritual and religious bases rather than on market-driven values, particularly the loss of meaning, loss of purpose, and loss of love undergirding much of public debate today. Helping individuals develop personal agency is not enough; pastoral counselors must also become involved politically to address how modernity impacts the conversations that individuals and families internalize.

The final chapter addresses the role of theological education in the formation of pastoral public theologians. It suggests that theological seminaries need to prepare their students for their public roles in ministry, no matter what the specific role they play within the life of the church or the community. The voice of the church must no longer be eclipsed in the marketplace. It needs to be heard as part of public debate.

Acknowledgments

Writing projects always come into existence because of a variety of influences and motivations. At the Melton Erickson Conference in Anaheim, California, in May 2000 I was exposed to the work of Michael White. His suggestion of working therapeutically with people who have been recruited into negative identities was pivotal to my understanding of counseling and therapy as political processes. I began to read the works of Michael White and apply his ideas to my understanding of African American pastoral care. Walter Earl Fluker, director of the Leadership Studies Center at Morehouse College, introduced me to the latest work in African American political science and religion, and he led me to the publication *New Day Begun: African American Churches and Civic Culture in Post–Civil Rights America.* It was this work that gave me inspiration to write this manuscript on the subject of the interface between the personal and socio-political dimensions of pastoral care. Memphis Theological Seminary and Eden Theological Seminary were key venues for trying out my ideas. The project Faith and the City, and especially its director, Doug Gatlin, helped me begin to think about how pastoral counseling makes a contribution to the public good. Monifa Jumanne, Constance Jackson, Lamont Wells, and Maisha Handy read portions of the manuscript in the process of its development. Michael A. Battle and Emmanual Lartey read portions of the manuscript and provided encouragement to continue. I am indebted to each of them for their support. I am also grateful to Robert Franklin for reading the manuscript and writing the foreword to it.

Chapter One

African American Pastoral Care and Counseling as Political Processes

HOMER ASHBY JR. sounds the battle cry for contemporary pastoral caregivers in *Our Home Is over Jordan*[1] when he painstakingly outlines the problems that African Americans face. He calls to our attention that the social and economic well-being of African Americans is only becoming worse, and that racial assault fueled by white supremacy is on the rise.[2] Unemployment of African Americans remains twice as high as that of whites. Many blacks seem to have withdrawn from fruitful involvement in politics. Homicide and AIDS, STDs, cancer, infant mortality, hypertension, and other illnesses are disproportionately represented among African Americans. And when it comes to how African Americans are portrayed in the media, Ashby says:

Two subtle messages are being sent to African Americans: Your insignificance as a participant in the cultural reality of America does not warrant portrayal on the television screen, and (2) your resentment and protest at being ignored is of little concern to us. In both ways African Americans are disregarded and made invisible.[3]

Ashby goes on to talk about other problems African Americans face, including nihilism or the loss of hope that threatens the emotional, spiritual, and physical well-being of African Americans. He discusses the internalized oppression that is at the heart of black-on-black crime and homicide rates, and cautions that a lack of a collective vision for the future among African Americans is leaving us very vulnerable.

Perhaps the most significant thing that Ashby lifts up as a threat to our survival as a people is our loss of a sense of community, our fragmentation as a people. Yes, we have become disconnected and disassociated from each other. We have lost a sense of peoplehood. We can no longer depend on our extended family ties and support systems to sustain us as they once did. Ashby's solution is to encourage us to rediscover the village or communities of care and nurture that will provide all the necessary ingredients for our healthy self-esteem. He says we need an ethic of care that "guides interpersonal relationships, fosters love, builds compassion, constructs systems of support, and denounces violence and abuse in all forms."[4]

As we might expect, he points to the black church as that vehicle for the recovery of the village, for the church embraces the larger plot that undergirds all activities of African American Christians and the wider community. For Ashby, it is in the recovery of our sense as an eschatological people working in partnership with God that we can hope to begin to rebuild our communities and enable African Americans to thrive.

Homer Ashby's program for reestablishing the village functions that once enabled us to thrive in a land of oppression is very important, for indeed without a communal vision we perish. In this book I suggest that we take another step toward healthy personal and communal functioning by acknowledging and drawing on pastoral counseling as an inherently political process that leads African Americans into full participation in the processes that shape their destiny as individuals and as a collective group.

This chapter has two aims. The first is to explore the meaning of pastoral counseling as a political process. The second aim is to examine how African American pastoral counseling has historically attended to the political and social transformation agenda and the link between the personal and public dimensions of life.

This book, then, is about pastoral counseling as a political process. By "political process" I mean the process that enables human beings to become fully involved and engaged in life so that each person can identify, develop, and exercise his or her full human capacities while at the same time enabling others to do likewise for the purpose of contributing to the common good. Participation in all life at all levels, which presupposes living in a democratic society, is what the political process is about. Thus, participating in how one's life and community are governed and administered is essential in the political process. Moreover, enabling people to participate in the political process of self-governing and community building is not a privilege but a God-given right, which God expects us to exercise even when that right is denied and obstacles to exercising it are erected. Pastoral counseling facilitates and enables persons to have the motivation and courage to engage, to get involved, to participate.

Contemporary efforts to limit the participation of African Americans in the political process of this nation take very subtle forms and are not limited by political party. It is not just the tampering with the Voting Rights Act, or making sure that our youth have criminal records, or the use of subtle or effective strategies to get young people to drop out of school that obliterate our chances of full participation. Rather, the process of political disenfranchisement subtly entices African Americans to internalize negative conversations, images, and stories about themselves such that there is no need for overt forms of racism. One such subtle mechanism is the negative portrayals of African Americans in the media, as Ashby also noted. Negative media portrayals stimulate internal conversations and lead us to deny our own worth and value, as well as to put down our own institutions and communities.

In this context of internalized racism, the role of pastoral counseling is to enable individuals, married couples, families, and mediating structures that bridge between the individual and the wider society to edit or re-author the negative internalized stories and identities that African Americans have embraced. The editing needs to facilitate and enable us to participate fully in society.

Such editing is understood as *a practice of the self* that enables individuals and small groups of people to alter the way they have been recruited into identities that are oppressive and self-destructive. Editing is also a *practice of care* exhibited by caregivers who create safe environments and provide help and prompting in understanding the evil of the past and the possibilities for the future that are necessary for persons to revise and re-author the internalized negative stories frustrating their growth and development.

Practices of the self and practices of care are inherently political processes. Political processes in a democracy by nature are oriented toward facilitating full participation in all of life, including the decision-making dimensions leading to community development and full employment of individual capacities and abilities. The ultimate aim of democratic political processes is to maximize individual and group participation in decision making in ways that benefit the common good. When the practices of self and the practices of care help to facilitate full participation in the democratic political processes of society, then they support full enfranchisement. While racial oppression seeks to limit and control the participation of African Americans in the decision-making processes through recruiting us into negative identities and stories, the practices of self and the practices of care facilitated by pastoral counseling have the power to undo the pejorative recruiting through editing processes.

The terms "practice of self" and "practices of care" are rooted in the practices of conversation and recruiting. These practices are seminal throughout this work. For Michel Foucault, it is discourse or conversation that makes practice intelligible. More specifically, practice provides a group of unifying rules that facilitate the interpretation of reality.[5] The practice of discourse or conversation establishes the order of speaking, the order with which we deal with words, the way we name reality, the way we analyze and classify things, and the way we explain things.

To illustrate how discourse or conversation sets priorities, let us look at the following words uttered in prayer by an elderly assistant pastor following a sermon I preached on September 19, 2004, at National Divine Spiritual Church in Atlanta:

God, we want you to bless the leaders of this nation, of this community, of this city, and this state. We do not want you to bless only Democrats or Republicans.

Rather, we want you to bless all of those in leadership regardless of political party. We ask this petition recognizing that we must ultimately turn to you, God, for all of our expectations. What we can expect from Democrats or Republicans is limited. But our expectations of you include things here on earth as well as things in heaven.

This elderly praying person had lived long enough to understand the limitations of political parties and what they can actually deliver when responding to the needs of people. He recognized that politics focus on scarce resources and that these resources are allocated based on who is in office or in power. Thus, he was helping listeners to understand that the response of political parties to human need is provisional at best. However, what we expect from God goes beyond scarce resources. Indeed, God's grace is unlimited and never scarce.

When this elderly man finished praying, I thought about the goals I was trying to accomplish in this writing project and how we orient our thinking and our lives toward conversations that we have with God and conversations we have in our faith communities. There is a lot to be derived from orienting our conversations toward God, since our identities as human beings come as a result of a gift from God. More precisely, society organizes its conversation based on the honor and shame categories of power, prestige, wealth, position, and privilege, and thus society allocates human worth and value according to those whom it deems worthwhile and honorable. However, God's granting of human worth and value is not limited to human categories of honor or shame, nor are they based on human achievement or merit. Consequently, the prayer of the elderly gentleman sought to orient us properly to God conversation, which is the ultimate source of our identity, worth, and value.

Orienting our conversation or discourse toward God is a mark of our belief about what is real, worthwhile, and valuable. Thus, we limit our expectations of what we can expect from Democrats or Republicans, and we participate in the political process knowing that we are strangers and foreigners on earth. Our highest goal is to reach an eternal home (Hebrews 13–16). This way of thinking about what is real is not only heavenly talk of "pie in the sky by and by." More precisely, this way of defining reality for African American Christians has been the way we have organized our expectations and our priorities.

Real power — political power — lies in the ability to control the practices of discourse and conversation. Moreover, real power enables selected groups of people to not only define reality but then recruit others into realities that may be alien to who they are. For example, the presidential race between incumbent George Bush and Senator John Kerry truly was a battle over who could define reality. Foucault says that the power to define reality is determined socially by who is accorded the right to speak first, the status of the one given the privilege to speak, their competence and knowledge, pedagogic norms, legal conditions, hierarchical attributions, and others; all these contribute to who gets the power to define what is real and not real.[6] The elderly man's prayer, however, helps us to recognize that political processes are conversations based on who can allocate scarce resources. Such political conversations are provisional and do not determine our worth and value as human beings. What we expect from political parties should be related to fair and just distribution of scarce resources, but we should never base our feelings of being worthwhile and valuable on who is in office or on political processes themselves. To do so would be practicing idolatry — that is, making political parties the ultimate grantor of human worth and value.

Thus, we must attend to the practices of discourse and the nature of what gets to be defined as real when we think of the political process. It is clear that skin color is one of the prime definers of who gets the power to speak first and to recruit others into their reality in the United States. Republicans generally do not want to deal publicly with statements about race and prefer to work behind the scenes on behalf of racial justice. Democrats prefer to talk publicly about race as a way to shore up their base within the black community. African Americans trust those politicians more who give open public assent to racial justice, and we distrust those politicians who do not. There are those within the black community, however, who are understandably suspicious of the democratic public pronouncements that are disingenuous and hollow.[7]

African American Christians have historically found their self-understanding in God, who is conceived as the ultimate definer of reality. Thus, many Christian African Americans rely more on their theological and faith convictions to orient them to what is real than on what is trumpeted by politicians. Within the African American Christian community, privileging conversation with God is what has given African Americans as individuals and as a group dignity and value that were denied by wider negative cultural images of us.[8]

Given our Christian theological bent, why should we attend to the political processes at all if the ultimate grantor of worth and value is God and not political parties or processes? One answer is that we still must be concerned about how scarce resources are allocated by political processes. We can participate, but we do so recognizing the limitation of such processes. Second, our faith teaches us that we must also express our faith in God and our response to God's gift of worth and value by doing acts of kindness that benefit the common good. Faith and works are united, as the book of James proclaims, and such a belief is rooted in African American convictions that fueled the antislavery movement.[9] So it is the practices of discourse rooted in the faith convictions of many African American Christians that define what is real and important as we participate in political power processes. Thus, we access the decision making that helps to facilitate full participation in all of life as a means of responding to our faith. We do so recognizing that such participation is important and essential, and yet that such participation is not the ultimate grantor of our worth and value as human beings. Political participation enhances God's gift of identity, but it is not the source of it.

Walter Fluker helps us to maintain the distinction between full participation in the political processes and the source of our true and underlying identity. He points out that African Americans sought full inclusion in the United States through the discourses and practices of civility, namely, the practices of recognition, respectability, and loyalty within their religion.[10] The practices of civility use the established rules of wider society to gain access to full participation in society. Yet Fluker shows that the practices of recognition, respectability, and loyalty become problematic if we do not keep in focus that our ultimate worth comes from God and not from practices that seek full acceptance from society. I reiterate: God bestows human worth on the least of these as well as on those whom society values the most. Fluker, however, is right to point out that the practices of civility are not without merit, in that they have the potential to build moral character as well as building up community.

Discourse is a political power process of defining reality. Thus, when African Americans are recruited into negative identities as a means of disenfranchising them, then African American pastoral counseling can step in as a political instrument for editing and undoing internalized oppression.

Therapy has often been thought of as serving the needs of the honor- and-shame culture of society and thus preserving existing racial and gender categories. Any notion that African American pastoral counseling functions to preserve the subordinate status of African Americans is erroneous. Instead, this book draws on Frederick C. Harris's notion that personal efficacy or agency is causally related to political efficacy; reminded through pastoral care and counseling of our personal and communal strength, we try to transform our lives through civic involvement.[11]

Four dimensions of African American pastoral counseling as a political process are our focus here. First, pastoral counseling liberates persons from those internalized conversations and stories into which they have been recruited that limit their full participation in the United States of America and prevent them from developing and exercising their full potential.

Second, pastoral counseling is a political process since it also attends to those mediating structures or institutions that stand between the individual's private sphere and wider cultural public institutions.[12] Mediating structures include those small meaning-making aggregations such as the family, church, voluntary associations, neighborhoods, and support systems that further the process of individuals' internalizing conversations. For Fluker, social networks and mediating structures provide social capital or community networks that enable community engagement that lead to political involvement. Thus, strengthening mediating structures enables African Americans to develop their full potential as well as to enable others to do the same. Pastoral counseling also functions to strengthen support systems that promote full engagement in life.

Third, pastoral counseling is political in the sense that it brings into the public arena insights from the actual counseling process. For example, one role of pastoral counseling in public theology is to bring a critique to modernity. Modernity is characterized by forces that disengage individuals from their communal roots and make them relational refugees.[13] When individuals are relational refugees, cut off from meaningful communal roots, they are more vulnerable to being recruited into negative identities and into conversations that disenfranchise them. Thus, pastoral counseling brings into the public debate over public policy those things that are needed to keep African Americans connected to each other and which build neighborhoods.

Finally, the practices of self are in themselves a political process. In the theory of discourse provided by Michel Foucault, caring for the self is an internal process that is connected with becoming an agent who is active in all of life. He calls this "the political game."[14]

African American Pastoral Counseling and Social Transformation

In the late 1960s and throughout the 1970s many African American intellectuals bemoaned the fact that the therapeutic movement in the United States had ignored the social agenda of African Americans and of other oppressed people. Black theological intellectuals called this exclusive attention to the personal and psychological aspects of therapy as "navel-gazing." They perceived psychotherapy to be burying its head in the sand, ignoring social ills, a practice completely irrelevant to the historical and social struggles of an oppressed people for liberation. Consequently, the therapeutic movement was relegated to the private dimensions of the lives of African Americans, and the real social and liberation agenda of African Americans belonged to the public domain. Thus, a split between the private and the public dimensions of ministry occurred.

More recently, the international community has leveled the same critique at the therapeutic movement. Emmanuel Y. Lartey has identified the different dimensions of the criticism.[15] As a black African, he recognizes that the therapeutic movement was a middle-class and ethnocentric movement that is slow to react to the socioeconomic position of women, ethnics, and other minorities. In fact, he says that the movement has been characterized by psychological reductionism, sociopolitical apathy, theological weakness, and individualism.[16] Psychological reductionism is the preference for psychological theories of human beings at the expense of social and cultural analysis. Social and political apathy relate to issues of economic and social power, marginalization, access, and social control that impact the lives of people and shape their experiences. The theological feebleness of which he speaks is the tendency of pastoral counseling to replace the faith orientation of Christianity with psychological models and individualism and to neglect the communal and interpersonal dimensions of the therapeutic whole.

As an alternative to the more traditional approach to therapy and pastoral counseling, Lartey has suggested a liberation model.[17] This model takes seriously the concrete experiences and the social location of the poor, the suffering, and the oppressed. Second, a social analysis of the conditions that impact and shape the experiences and lives of the poor, suffering, oppressed, and marginalized are addressed. Third, the theological feebleness of pastoral counseling is addressed by helping the poor and oppressed to interpret and reinterpret their human condition in light of sacred scriptures. Finally, he sees pastoral counseling as the liberation praxis where people in groups encounter each other seeking social transformation of their situation. This latter phase is what he calls symbolic collective action — such as marches, protests, and demonstrations — by the poor that calls attention to the issues that impact their lives.[18]

More recently among African American theological intellectuals, however, there is a fermenting of thought that is gaining a healthy respect for the role of the therapeutic in the lives of African Americans. Echoing much of the similar critique as Lartey, Cornel West has critically examined the social situation that many African Americans are in today. He points out that the cultural structures that once supported black life are collapsing all around.[19] He critiques both liberals and conservatives for ignoring the despair and dread that flood the streets of black America, posing a threat to our very existence. West recognizes that nihilism is more than economic deprivation and political powerlessness. He writes, "It is primarily a question of speaking to the profound sense of psychological depression, personal wholeness, and social despair so widespread in black America."[20] West points out that oppressed people are starving for identity, meaning, and self-worth. He recognizes that too much attention to the social political realities of black people often means neglecting personal dimensions, and that this contributes to the nihilism or the loss of love, meaning, and purpose. Thus, West calls for the political and the therapeutic to join forces to address not only the sociopolitical agenda of liberation, but also the nihilism that is eclipsing the social and racial progress of African Americans.

Within African American pastoral theology, several voices have emerged that link the ethical/political dimensions with the pastoral. Key in these emerging voices is a view of the self as active rather than passive, a self that has the capacity of transforming itself and others despite the presence of oppression and racism. As early as 1982, Archie Smith explored the relationship of liberation ethics and the practice of psychotherapy.[21] He considered ethics as our response to God's divine liberation activity through action and reflection on God's liberation activity. He built on the concept of the relational self as an agent in the liberation struggle as well as in the authoring of one's own life.[22] Thus, he contended, the self need not be a victim of oppression, but can actively get in-volved in the transformation of self and others despite racism and oppression. Thus, Smith says:

> Since society and the self are interrelated and interwo-ven realities, both social ethics and therapy may be seen as part of a praxis that understands social transforma-tion and psychic liberation to be inseparable. Social ethics and therapy employ a reflexive, self-critical methodology which seeks to free human life from fetishism and idola-trous forms of faith and to enable people to reconstitute themselves in light of new self-understanding of a just and liberating social order.[23]

From her particular perspective, Carroll Watkins Ali draws on African American women's experience to focus on the tasks of survival and liberation.[24] For her, survival is the ca-pacity to resist systematic oppression and genocide and to recover the self from abuse and dehumanization. Liberation is total freedom from oppression and the ability to engage in the transformation of oppressive culture through political resistance.

Elaine Crawford, a womanist theologian, also lifts up the concept of the agency of self in the face of oppression.[25] She sees the transformative process of the engagement of the self with God using the creative power of reinterpretation of scrip-ture as being key to gaining new and liberating perspective on one's self and its relationship to society. Here again the self becomes an agent in the transformation of self and in society.

Carolyn McCrary explores the concept of internalized op-pression and how such oppression functions at a depth level in African Americans.[26] She builds on the depth psychological perspective of the British school of psychoanalysis and object relations theory to explicate the power that internalized oppression has on the interior lives of African Americans. For her, internalized oppression results from internalized negative relationships that sabotage personal growth. Therapy then enables internalized oppressive relationships to be replaced by liberating and nurturing ones as the counselee uses the therapist as transitional internalized support to transform existing negative inner relationships.

Homer Ashby is another pastoral theologian who develops the notion of the self as an agent through the concept of home not as a place, but as an attitude that enables African Americans to be at home in the world by engagement with the biblical story and political transformation of space.[27] The process of being at home in a strange land is an interior process involving practices for the recovery of the self and for self-formation, yet the process of interiority is not unrelated to the external process of liberation. Drawing on Watkins Ali's distinction between survival and liberation he says:

> These concrete actions flow from the interior process of self-formation and make themselves manifest in exterior campaigns of liberation. Understood in this way survival is a necessary precursor to liberation. Without a clear sense of identity and destiny it is impossible to act with the necessary internal fortitude to engage in resistance and transformation. A prerequisite to liberation is time and energy devoted to the survival functions. The liberation function rests upon the survival functions in order to bring them to full and satisfactory completion.[28]

For him, then, the survival function, which involves the recovery of identity and of the self, eventuates in political action. Thus, liberation and survival functions are interrelated. In his mind, part of the problem with African Americans in the twenty-first century is the exclusive attention to the liberation function without attending to the survival function.

This chapter has introduced the idea that African American pastoral counseling is inherently a political process that leads African Americans into full participation in shaping their own destiny. Pastoral counseling also operates as a political process in that it attends to the ways in which African Americans have been recruited into negative self-images that destroy human agency and prevent full participation in society. African American pastoral counseling draws on the practices of self and care in the editing process. The practices of the self and care are grounded in the notion of conversation and discourse, which inform what people internalize. African American pastoral counseling has become a countercultural movement because it orients African American Christians toward the ultimate grantor of worth and value: God. As a result, the source of identity and meaning in life shifts away from the honor and shame norms of wider culture.

To a great extent, African American pastoral counseling tries to show the limitations of the political process in the allocation of scarce resources. Though necessary, the importance of political processes for granting worth and dignity must always be tempered by the reality that worth and dignity are gifts from God.

African American pastoral counseling helps us to develop human agency in the direction of contributing to the common good not as a way to earn dignity. Rather, our development of agency and our participation in acts of kindness and justice are attempts to respond to the gift of worth and dignity from God. It is a response to God's love manifested in Jesus Christ.

Finally, African American pastoral counseling has historically attended to the political and social agenda impacting African Americans. What is different today is that the voices of African American pastoral counselors will be heeded more because the restoration of village functions in the African American community and the linking of personal agency with political efficacy pull pastoral counselors into public debate.

◆ *Chapter Two* ◆

The Parish Context of African American Pastoral Counseling

W E EACH BUILD the foundation for becoming a self and for developing personal agency through the conversations we internalize in whatever families and networks of relationships we are raised. This chapter looks particularly at the local congregation as an original meaning-making environment, an environment that provides foundational practices for the development of the self. It also explores graduate theological education as a shaping environment for understanding pastoral counseling as a political process.

Pastoral Counseling and the Home

As a boy growing up in a small southern New Jersey home, I used to watch my father accompany people through our living room to his study. My father, a pastor of a small Methodist church, was particularly adept as a pastoral counselor. He had spent many years taking courses and volunteering in hospitals when the pastoral care movement was just attaining credibility in the early 1950s. At the time I witnessed the people tracking through our living room, I had no idea what was going on in the study, though I did surmise that there were some significant and serious conversations taking place between my father and parishioners. Not until much later did I begin to realize that my father was providing pastoral counseling to people, and this realization identified for me the actual source of my initiation into both the profession of pastoral counseling and my understanding of being called to a ministry primarily of pastoral counseling.

But as a child, I was not simply an observer of my father's ministry: I was also privileged to accompany my father on some of his pastoral visitations to parishioners' homes. My father would begin taking Holy Communion to the sick and shut-ins on the first Sunday of each month, and he would continue the rest of that week until he had completed visiting all of those who were not able to come to church. Most of the time, I would be allowed to come inside and watch the activity, but on those occasions that I would be asked to leave I understood that some serious conversation between grown-ups was about to take place at which it would be best if I were not present. Whether hearing the conversations or not, I was being shaped by my father's practice of ministry. For example, my father was always attentive to greetings and finding out about how the parishioners were feeling. He would always engage in conversations with parishioners before he gave them communion. And so I learned the vital importance of attending to people's needs by listening to their stories about life.

Such experiences became the first source of both my knowledge of and skills in pastoral care and counseling. That my primary profession and orientation to work was formed very early in my development prior to most of my formal education is both immensely satisfying and eye-opening.

And there were other such occasions, part of our everyday household activities — occasions for learning pastoral counseling skills by overhearing my parents' dinnertime bantering about the nature of counseling. My mother would say to my father, "You don't know anything about counseling," Quickly adding, "Counseling is not giving advice." My father would respond with just as much assurance and speed: "I don't give advice."

Such brief exchanges between my father and mother reflected the wider academic conversation taking place in the profession of counseling and pastoral counseling. In the 1950s Carl Rogers made popular the notion of nondirective counseling. Rogers cautioned against advice giving and directive approaches to counseling; he urged counselors to employ empathy and trust of the counselees' inner direction in helping the counselee achieve his or her therapeutic goals. To some extent, Rogers was revising his own understanding of what many ministers did in counseling as he saw it; his father was a minister, and he grew up in a parsonage. Rogers's life work was to put in secular language the theological understanding and meaning of self-giving and selfless love. He called such love "unconditional positive regard" and "entering into the internal frame of reference" of the counselee.

My childhood and youth were privileged in that I was a willing witness to this debate about the difference between pastoral counseling as direction and pastoral counseling as nondirective conversation between pastoral counselor and counselee, played out both by my parents and by the field. My mother represented the nondirective, empathic Rogerian perspective, my father the more traditional and directive approach. At the time my maturational age did not permit me to appreciate in any depth what I was learning experientially by listening to my parents' conversation. Nonetheless, a significant foundation was being laid that would propel me naturally into the profession of pastoral counseling.

Part of this natural propulsion was the fact that my mother was a guidance counselor in the Philadelphia public school system, while my father was a pastor and began to attend pastoral counseling classes at what was then known as Temple University School of Theology (later Conwell School of Theology at Temple University). My original formation environment provided the basic foundation for knowledge and skills in counseling that made it easier for me to enter into professional and academic counseling. What I had internalized from my childhood formation surfaced later to be developed into my approach to pastoral care and counseling, which I subsequently called African American pastoral care and counseling.

This formational environment I later mined for nuggets of wisdom. For example, my mother's understanding of counseling came from her training in social work and guidance and counseling. Her understanding of counseling was deeply Rogerian, believing in the capacity of each person to actualize his or her full possibilities given the right supportive emotional environment. On the other hand, my father's understanding of counseling came from experiences in parish ministry as well as from his courses in pastoral counseling in the 1950s and 1960s, when pastoral counseling was becoming part of theological education. He believed in the role of the pastor as a guide who gave wisdom about problems without taking over the decision-making process. He did not mind being active and direct in sharing his wisdom. My father saw the value of counseling psychology for his role as a parish pastor. He understood the role of empathy and attending to the internal frame of the person in creating relationships with parishioners, yet he also knew that he had the freedom to help people to solve problems and to suggest practical solutions. What strikes me now about the conversational environment of my childhood is the fact that my father seemed to be able to capture the essence of counseling, which is empathy, and to use it in his work as a pastor who made strategic intervention with concrete ideas about how to solve problems.

My mother's critique was the fact that my father was not a Rogerian purist. She was correct. He made his parish context central in that he was the leader who offered direction and guidance, yet he did so without making parishioners children. He also took seriously their feelings and their own points of view about their problems. In short, he drew from counseling theory only those ideas and principles he needed to help empower people within his parish.

The context in which one works and lives informs what one does in counseling, I learned. The educational guidance counseling movement and social work contextual world influenced what my mother did with her schoolchildren and youth. What my father did with counseling was also shaped by his work as a pastor in an African American and Methodist context. For example, I recall how my father shared his wisdom with my wife when we lost our first child, who was born two months prematurely — a difficult situation for both of us. My father was very empathic with the loss both of us felt, but it was his sharing of wisdom with my wife that made her have hope. He said at one point that Diana Key, as we named our child, was now with God. He said she came from God and now she was back with God. For my wife, the conversation and my father's words were the funeral and the eulogy that we never had. She felt my dad understood just what she needed emotionally as well as spiritually. His direct words were comforting and offered her a new framework for understanding our loss, one that presented a hopeful perspective.

My mother, on the other hand, besides being empathic, would draw on non-directive-oriented counseling. For example, she would always ask evocative questions that got others to think deeply about their problems without offering much in the way of advice or suggestions. My father, however, employed empathy along with being more direct and sharing his wisdom and also stories.

The practice of counseling is influenced by the knowledge and skills that are implied in the practice of counseling within particular contexts. Michel Foucault is correct because he emphasized that discourse or conversation is an act or event that forms a complete meaning system, and it shapes behavior. Moreover, attention to discourse or conversation also reveals much about the practices that shape professional identity.[1] Indeed, our original conversational environment provides all the knowledge and skills we need to engage in everyday and professional life. What we must do, however, is to mine what is learned from these original contexts in our professional education.

The family of origin or our family of birth is the primary meaning-making environment that provides the original context where our primary needs are met. As infants, we are born into a world that is rich in conversation and discourse as well as in relationships. Originally, we don't have the capacity to participate in conversations, but we have the ability through our relationships with others to catch felt meaning and impressions. As a result, we are then able to form these into words, sentences, and stories as we grow through the life cycle.

Our capacity for internalizing relationships and attitudes of others is basic to our existence as persons, and the quality of relationships with others enables us to feel loved, cared for, worthwhile, and valued at a very basic level of our existence as infants. Later in our growth and development the felt impressions formed prior to language make up the foundation, which becomes the source of our identity and personality. At the same time we begin to use words, sentences, and stories to understand ourselves as we develop the cognitive capacities to think, reflect, and tell and retell stories.

The family of origin, the family of birth, the family of creation, and the family of rearing are our first memberships in community, and the things learned in these early membership contexts become foundational for us. Thus, the lessons learned in them must be attended to when we begin to think about what influences our basic understanding of reality.

Such reflecting back on our original meaning-making contexts is more than mere reflection; it is a practice of remembering in which we identify and acknowledge those persons who contributed significantly to the stories that shaped our identities, our knowledge of ourselves and of the world, and the skills that we employ in dealing with others and the world.[2] To recall and to remember stories that shaped our lives in our original meaning-making contexts contribute to our ongoing development and ability to further our identity development as well as continuing to develop the vocation to which we have been called.

For me, a significant example of using the wisdom of the past in the present is the work I am currently doing in spiritual renewal. As a child, my father would tell the congregation his call story at least twice a year. I remember his call story very well. At the time I heard it as a youth, it provided me with the expectation that I would possibly be called to the ministry in a similar way as my father. My own call, however, was different in that my call was not dramatic. I just became aware at sixteen that I wanted to be in ministry. My call was influenced by a group of youth who insisted that I bring the word of God one evening at our youth camp. While I resisted mightily, they insisted just as vigorously.

In the mid-1990s following my heart surgery I revisited my childhood memories of Father's call story. I was flat on my back for at least a week, and I had eight weeks to spend in recovery. I used the time as a spiritual retreat to listen to God, and the result was a reorientation in the way I lived my life. I became a vegetarian, and I knew I had to live my life risking more intimacy with my wife, since I discovered that fear of intimacy is often a major factor in clogging arteries.

My heart problems came during my midlife crises. I realized in resolving my midlife crisis that my father told his call story at times when he needed to be reminded of why he chose ministry as his life's work. As a means of spiritual renewal, I subsequently began to develop workshops based on how my father recalled his call story. My publication of the book *Recalling Our Own Stories: Spiritual Renewal for Religious Caregivers* was the result.[3] Periodically, I also return to my own call story as a way to renew my life. More recently, I have begun to recall my miraculous recovery from bypass surgery as my second call story. My father's pattern of recalling his call story is something I employ constantly as a means of renewal as well as a means of sharing with others.

From these original contexts we encounter local discourses and communities of wisdom, which then are often disqualified and relegated by some contemporary perspectives as invalid folk wisdom that is useless in negotiating life. We are discovering that our original contexts of meaning are essential to the way we live today, and to marginalize them and render them useless severely handicaps our abilities to participate in life at all levels. In other words, recalling practices that lead us to remember the original shaping influences in our lives helps to facilitate our full participation in life at all levels. In short, our ability to exercise our political agency that leads to full participation in life involves revisiting those original meaning-generating contexts associated with our families of origin and birth.

The Parish and Pastoral Counseling

I became the pastor of a local congregation in 1966. I was in my second year of theological education. In 1968, at the end of my seminary education, I went to another congregation, which I served until 1974. My first congregation was an all-white congregation in a small town in central Massachusetts near the New Hampshire boarder. My second congregation was African American in a city environment in central Massachusetts, which I served until I completed my doctorate in philosophy. In both congregations I learned a great deal about the political meaning of pastoral counseling.

So I began my pastoral ministry in 1966 in a small town in central Massachusetts, and shortly after, in the fall of 1967 embarked on my first Clinical Pastoral Education (CPE) experience at Boston State Hospital. The Vietnam War was very prominent, and it was the subject matter of many of our classes. The small town in which I was the pastor had five churches, and the veterans organizations were strong. The townspeople took their patriotism very seriously.

My congregation was a joint venture of two different congregations that had joined together because of declining populations. One congregation was United Methodist, and the other congregation was Episcopal. Most of the congregants were retired, although there were a few young and middle-aged couples in the church. To my surprise, many were conservative Republicans; prior to coming to this town, I had thought that all people in the world were New Deal Democrats! For the first time I met people who thought that Franklin D. Roosevelt was the worst person on earth because of his economic policies.

Another segment of the congregation was a group of seventy or so young boys who attended a local boarding high school. The Vietnam War was on their minds. While in seminary, we were urged to address the Vietnam War from the pulpit because many felt we should end this war for a variety of reasons. Given the youth and their eventually having to enter the draft, I decided to take a stand from the pulpit against the Vietnam War. I was about to embark on my first real lesson about the nature of politics and its relationship to pastoral care and counseling.

Not long into my sermon on Vietnam, one of the older ladies of the congregation stood up and rushed out of the church. I could not miss the fact that she was very upset and disturbed about what I was saying. I was shocked at her leaving; it rattled me, and I had difficulty completing my sermon without reading it word for word. I did not know what to do or where to turn. My assumption had been that the Vietnam War was unpopular for everybody.

The very next day I went to Boston for my CPE class. In my school reflection group, I brought up what had happened the previous day in church. My clinical supervisor told me to go visit the woman who walked out of the church and to be open to what I would learn. I went, and she gave me an earful about how she felt and why she thought I had committed an unpardonable sin.

This woman had spent all of her adult life as a school-teacher, and she had had to resign recently due to an incapacitating illness. She indicated that her meaning in life was derived from teaching her young students that "it was my country right or wrong." What I had done was very offensive to her; I had undermined her reason for teaching all those many years.

What surprised me was the fact that I was not able to leave this woman's home for over three hours. In time, I came to find out that she was very lonely, and she appreciated my visits and looked forward to them. Although we differed politically, she thought of herself as a teacher of this young black male in his first pastorate who needed to be educated about how things really are in the world and in that community. My visits helped her to express her deep feelings of loss and also helped her to find meaning in what she could actually do with her life without teaching. In short, I was helping her to find other avenues of meaning making, and she in turn taught me to question my assumptions.

My experience with this woman was a critical lesson in recognizing that pastoral counseling enables people to participate meaningfully in life. Part of the political process is enabling everyone to participate in life as fully as they are able. When obstacles occur, whether they are the result of racial discrimination or incapacitating illness, the practices of care motivate people to keep on "keeping on" despite the circumstances and to find meaningful avenues of participation. This is the true meaning of the political process: the capacity to participate to our fullest ability in life and in decision making.

In this small congregation I learned that the practices of care had empowering possibilities. In 1968 Martin Luther King was assassinated while I was pastor of this congregation. Immediately, the town responded. My wife and I had a steady flow of visitors from my congregation and from the town's people. They were profoundly impacted by the murder of Dr. King. Immediately, I was asked to do a memorial service at my church and to preach a memorial service honoring Dr. King.

These stories that I have told from my family of origin and my first parish show how I began to learn how pastoral counseling is a political process. These original contexts are all communities of close kinship networks, whether blood or fictive ties, and communities of daily support that help us maintain our emotional, interpersonal, and physical integrity as persons. Such networks include not only our families and extended families; they also include voluntary associations like churches, neighborhood associations, and small groupings in which we encounter others on a daily bases.

These communities of original membership provide vital environments and contexts for dynamic and meaningful conversations and discourses that shape our primary orientation to life. Such conversations tell us what is significant and important to life and inform how we live, move, and act in the world. They define for us how we relate to ourselves and to others. They give us clues to what we should internalize from wider culture, and they help us navigate the many conversations that we hear in our lives. These original environments help us shape the overarching meaning system or framework for our convictions and beliefs: who we are as human beings, how we are to relate to others, and how we are to participate in life at all levels. Such a conversational convictional system provides us with messages that inform our worth and value as human beings: they tell us why we are here, what our calling is in life, and how we should negotiate the world outside of our original memberships and formation contexts. In addition, these original contexts model conversational practices, which also help to orient us to what is significant for making meaning in our lives and to have similar conversations ourselves.

In brief, our original membership communities represent social capital or a reservoir of resources on which to draw, enabling full participation in life. Moreover, these original membership communities are mediating structures that stand between the individual and wider society. The role of these mediating structures is to modify the conversational messages of wider society so that they facilitate authentic and meaningful participating in life.

Mining Original Knowledge in Professional Education and the Political Process

In addition to pastoral care in the parish setting, I also learned about pastoral care in graduate professional education. There was a major crisis in my work on the PhD when I was working at the Danielsen Pastoral Counseling Center at Boston University. When I entered the PhD program at Boston University Graduate School in 1971, I had already completed two years of pastoral counseling training at the Worcester Area Council of Churches. I was steeped in Rogerian therapy; I had thoroughly embraced my mother's side of the counseling tradition. The crisis came when I took my performance examination. My professors and supervisors told me that I was not a Rogerian, and that I needed to return to my counseling and try to become more authentic, more fully myself. In other words, they saw a side of me that related to the way my father had integrated counseling into his pastoral identity, and they wanted me to get in touch with this side of me so that my approach to pastoral counseling resonated fully, not only partly, with who I was, how I understood myself, what I had learned from my original family and parish learning contexts. Essentially I was being told to do what Michael White calls re-membership, or returning to our original knowledge and skills learned in early conversational environments.[4] Not only was I given permission to embrace my past, I was also being empowered to actualize who I truly was as a human being and to use it as I participated fully in the academic process. Thanks to their prompting and their insistence, I was learning what political empowerment was all about: discovering the gifts that I had as a human being and using them to make a place for myself and others in society.

To be empowered to the fullest, I had to learn how I presented myself to the world. When I was growing up, I was a very poor student. In fact, I did not learn to read until I was in the eighth grade. My inability to read was hampered by both internal and external processes. The internal processes, I came to learn, were related to the personality character disorder known as passive aggressiveness. Passive aggressiveness is a behavioral pattern where anger is neither expressed openly nor directly. Rather, anger goes underground and is expressed through stubbornness and sullen attitudes, and through inefficiency and procrastination. All are strategies used to defeat authority figures.[5] The hallmark strategy used by many passive-aggressive children is the inability to read. For me, having parents who were highly educated and who had high academic expectations was a threat to my own sense of power. Thus, I unconsciously felt that I had to defeat them in order for me to have any autonomy at all.

I mention passive aggressiveness not only because it was an unconscious pattern I used to handle my anger; I lift it up also because it was a convenient cultural pattern that was used by many African American males in pre–civil rights days. One could lose one's life if anger was expressed openly. Anger is a source of personal agency if used properly and constructively, and anger could be channeled in ways that challenged the racial structures and conversations that disempowered African Americans. Thus, any sign of anger, whether constructive or not, would be confronted by whites.

So in fact by being passive aggressive and not learning to read I was disempowering myself. I was not presenting myself authentically to the world, although I would survive and live a long life as a black male. Thus, my first lesson in empowerment came when I realized that I had to claim and demonstrate the intelligence that I actually had and use it proactively.

Pastoral counseling training and my work toward the PhD in pastoral psychology and counseling helped me to claim my intellectual gifts and to mine lessons my parents tried to teach me earlier, which I had been too stubborn to learn then. First, my parents told me that intelligence was not a gift that only a few possessed — as whites insisted. My parents said over and over again that intelligence came as the result of hard work and study. Second, they insisted that I was intelligent, but that I refused to use my intelligence. Pastoral counseling training pointed out that one of my patterns of negotiating the world was to put myself down, falsely presenting myself to the world. My supervisors indicated that I was not playing fair by letting others think that I was not intelligent or less than what I was. They challenged me to present my real self to others, and this was the road to full empowerment. They said I had to risk being myself no matter the consequences; this was the only true way to live.

Not claiming my gifts and intelligence was an unfair game to play. It was my way of consciously determining who was a racist. Racists would automatically buy into the way I initially defined myself without ever trying to find out who I really was. Nonracists would look beyond my initial self-presentation to see who I really was. Nonracists would eventually see who I was and embrace who I was, so I reasoned.

Pastoral counseling taught me to be proactive about how I wanted to be seen by others. I learned not to wait for permission to be myself. Rather, I learned that I was in charge of how I wanted the world to see me. Thus, being an authentic self became a political act of empowerment given the nature of racism in the United States.

The problems that I had in reading also had a legacy in slavery. Learning to read in the cultural climate of slavery was forbidden. Although I was far removed from slavery in that I was born in 1943, the fact that I had a twisted understanding of intelligence despite my parents' conscious attempt to counteract it proves that the cultural legacy of inferiority and superiority surrounding intelligence survived slavery, and I had learned it well.[6] I actually internalized as a child the conviction that real intelligence was a gift that I did not have, and only the gifted had it. I was not one of the gifted people, and neither were my peers. Thus, my own convictional structure disempowered me.

Several learning experiences in the classroom in graduate school helped me to edit my internalized oppression. The first was a course in psychological measurement where I learned about how intelligence was measured. The second was reading Carl Jung's book called *Psychology and Education;* the third relates to understanding the multiple levels of intelligence beyond the emphasis on just intellectual intelligence. The language for talking about multiple levels of intelligence comes from the contemporary movement known as emotional intelligence.

My convictional or belief structure, which was challenged by graduate school, was well established by the time I went to college and graduate school. I grew up in a community context where the dominant cultural conversation driving education was a belief in the inherent inferiority of African Americans. While the message of the innate inferiority of African Americans became explicit at times, the way my peers and I internalized this message was very subtle and hardly conscious. For example, we believed that being smart was an innate gift with which one was born. If one were not gifted from birth, one was predestined to being a mediocre or poor student, and therefore, one person should not try hard to obtain educational things that were out of one's grasp. In my school environment, this belief was never openly challenged, and the really gifted students sat in the front of the class, and the mediocre and less gifted students sat in the back of the class.

Of course, I sat in the back of the class believing that I was an average student at best. My father, however, understood how racism worked, and he set out to convince me that I was neither stupid nor average. I remember one incident in the seventh grade, where he called me to his study. He then locked the door and said, "Not one of us will be leaving this study until you realize you are not stupid and that learning is a matter of hard work." Of course, I resisted, but at the end of the day I knew I could learn. He had begun his professional career as a teacher in Florida when segregation was at its highest point in the 1930s, and had long since understood how many students had internalized the dominant conversation of racial inferiority.

The congregation that my father served also tried to counter the racial myth of intellectual inferiority. My Sunday school teacher never believed that my poor reading was due to poor intelligence. She always encouraged me by offering alternative explanations for my poor reading skills.

Because of my father, my Sunday school teacher, and some other teachers along the way, I did internalize an alternative message about learning. Learning was hard work, yet I was capable of doing far more academically than I had earlier understood or believed. It was not until I was working on my doctor of philosophy degree, however, that I began to find theoretical evidence for what my father and church people were saying about intelligence. I took a course in psychological testing and measurement. We had to actually buy the standardized intelligence tests that were administered at that time. We also had to order the explanations about the statistical reliability and validity of each test question. In the process, I learned that each test question was based on concrete but subtle intellectual skills that were not innate, but which could be actually practiced and learned. My high school football coach used to say this, and he urged the African American football players to begin taking the SAT test in the tenth grade like the white students did. Yet most of us did not pay any attention to him. His point was that these tests were not so much aptitude tests measuring innate intelligence but achievement tests focusing on real skills that were taught and reinforced within the educational environment of the school.

It was only when I saw the concrete examples of how intelligence tests are created that I finally accepted that learning was more about hard work and achievement than innate intelligence. Consequently, the mystifying and intimidating belief that whites were innately intellectually superior to black people was finally toppled.

I also learned another significant thing about intelligence while preparing for my German language exam for my PhD. I had to read Carl Jung's book *Psychology of Education* in its original German and be tested on interpreting a passage in it.[7] Chapter 4 is about the gifted child, and this book gave me an understanding of the multiple natures of human intelligence beyond the debate in the United States confining intelligence only to intellectual intelligence. What Jung taught me was that intelligence is more than technical or rational, and it includes what Jung calls the emotional and ethical dimensions.[8] In his essay "The Gifted Child"[9] he says that there are gifts of the mind and gifts of the heart. He summarizes his convictions about intelligence by drawing on his profession as a psychotherapist. He concludes: "Psychotherapy has taught us that in the final reckoning it is not knowledge, not technical skill that has curative effect, but the personality of the doctor. And it is the same with education: it presupposes self-education."[10]

He goes on to say that gifts of intelligence can be used to the extent that the personality grows and develops, and that intelligence is multileveled. Accepting this fact enabled me to embrace my own gifts of intelligence. My formal education at the graduate level opened me to different understandings of intelligence in general and my intelligence in particular that propelled me beyond internalized racist notions of my intellectual inferiority.

My family of origin, my church, and my educational experiences in graduate school helped me to edit wider racist cultural expectations that would have disenfranchised me from full participation in society. Racism by its very nature is political in that it seeks to exclude people from full participation in society by recruiting them into negative stories, plots, and images. Whenever these pejorative images, plots, and stories are challenged and transformed through editing, liberation to be full participants in society at all levels is taking place.

The point of dealing with one's own internalized racism is extremely important, because it helps us to do two things on the structural level. Racism is structural where avenues for full participation in society are systemically cut off. Racism is also symbolic: it exists at the levels of cultural symbols that inform the conversations and ideas we internalize. When structural racism is addressed and eliminated at the policy level, however, racism can still exist at the symbolic level. Thus, symbolic-level racism keeps us in bondage even if structural racism disappears. It is our challenge to help people continue editing their lives.

Some Final Comments on the Congregational/Parish Context of Pastoral Counseling

It is clear that my original memberships in local congregations shaped my understanding of racism and how to deal with it at the symbolic and structural levels. The question remains, however: what conclusions can be drawn for the role of pastoral counseling as a political process that grows out of the parish context? Pastoral counseling that takes place within the context of a local African American congregation is influenced by the dominant beliefs and convictions of that congregation, particularly about the nature of human beings and about the way human beings are empowered to participate in society. Two examples can make this case.

First, Alice Wiley, a former doctor of ministry student whose dissertation committee I chaired, helped me to visualize that pastoral counseling practiced within a local congregation takes on the dominant convictions and beliefs of that local congregation. She demonstrated in her dissertation how certain womanist values espoused in a local congregation, of which she and her husband were pastors, shaped the development of a pastoral counseling center within their church. Key in her dissertation were relational values of care and nurture and how important they were in empowering others. She talked about how she prepared her congregation for the counseling center by preaching sermons reflecting the womanist values of relationships and caring and how they were outgrowths of the role of women in extended families and in the life of local churches. She concluded that the convictions and values of that congregation permeated the whole center, particularly because the trained counselors were recruited from the church's membership.[11]

A second example that confirms the fact that pastoral counseling within a parish context takes on the values of the congregation is made by a story that Don Browning includes in one of his publications, *A Fundamental Practical Theology: Descriptive and Strategic Proposals*. It is an example of the congregational care program of a local African American Pentecostal congregation.[12]

The congregational care is carried out by many groups and departments of that congregation. The pastor delegates responsibilities, but he also supervises the caring activities. His supervision includes creating a shared theology and ethics of care among all who participate in the program. "Many important religious beliefs and values are communicated by the way we care for one another," says the pastor.[13] The caring ministries include lay ministers who visit the sick in hospitals and the elderly in nursing homes, take communion to shut-ins, and staff the prayer phone lines. There were also outreach ministries to prisons and to projects where the poor lived. Browning concludes his observations on the relationship of the caring practices of the congregation with its beliefs and convictions in the following way:

> Given this part of my background, it surprised me to see the extent of psychological language, insights, and attitudes in this African American Pentecostal church. The number of mental health professionals, school counselors, social workers, and teaches trained in psychology far

exceeded my expectations. But the moral and theological framework that guided the use of these psychologies was not the framework of most mainline Protestant churches. There was not "triumph of the therapeutic," to use Reiff's felicitous phrase, at the Apostolic Church.

In his preaching, teaching, and example Brazier (the pastor) set the theological and ethical framework for using the modern psychologies. Yet it grew out of the similarities between his experience and the experiences of his people in the inner city and in their congregation with Scripture.[14]

Browning goes on to say that the ethical framework for using modern psychologies was clearly related to married couples, families, and the task of raising children rather than individualism or ethical egoism. The concern was the significance of the black family and its reconstruction. But there was also a strong ministry to singles.[15]

The manner in which convictions and beliefs are espoused within the life of the church impacts the way ministries of care are carried out. Although the church was Pentecostal, there was a great concern for developing persons for outreach to the community. Becoming productive citizens and contributing to the common good were what Christians were supposed to be about. The congregation was also concerned to connect church work with community organizations in order to bring low- and moderate-income housing to the community, to improve local schools, to fight drugs, and to bring businesses and banks to the local community. Although there is a liberation theology, this theology is subservient to the theology of salvation and redemption, according to Browning.[16]

This approach is important to demonstrate that evangelical theology can engage and lead to full participation in society, just as liberation theologies do. Social outreach and political activism cut across theological lines. The family and the local congregation are vital contexts for providing meaningful conversations that can be drawn on for a lifetime. The original shaping contexts provide significant resources to support our full participation in life using all of our gifts.

Chapter Three

Liberation from Oppressive Conversations

THE CHAPTER has two aims. The first is to explore how being recruited into negative identities is a political act. The second is to demonstrate how the practices of lament, participation in God (sapience), connecting with others, transparency, editing of negative identities, and other practices lead to political efficacy.

To accomplish the aims of this chapter, I present case studies from the lives of three people: E. Lynn Harris, noted author; Linda Hollies, author and minister; and Wilson Goode, former mayor of Philadelphia.

Healing in the Life of E. Lynn Harris

E. Lynn Harris has become famous for his novels that address the lives of men who struggle with their male sexual identities. While his novels are not autobiographical, he himself has struggled with sense of worth, and has found affirmation and value in God and in his work. He talks about his pilgrimage to wholeness in his memoirs entitled *What Becomes of the Brokenhearted.*[1]

Harris begins his memoirs by acknowledging the significance of God in his life. He says, "This author is grateful to God for waking me up each morning and allowing me to have a career I love and have a great deal of passion for it."[2] These are the words of a man who has actualized a great deal of his possibilities as a human being and who participates fully in society to the extent of his true capabilities. Moreover, he has embarked on a career that is enabling many others to accept and love themselves through his writing. He is a man with personal agency, and he is using his agency to empower others toward the end of full participation in society as well. The source of his personal power, which has become personal agency and political efficacy, is his relationship with God. This relationship with God has provided him with a sense of self-acceptance despite his self-hatred, and it was God's guidance and support that helped him get through the most difficult time of his life. It was also God who enabled him to deal with the way in which he was violently recruited into an identity and a story that was not of his own creation.

Harris begins his memoirs with a complaint to God. He believed that God was deliberately distant from him, and he desperately desired God's closeness and love to be made known to him. He writes:

> I mumbled on for a few minutes about how bad my life was; they told me to trust in God and pray. I told them I would try to feel better, even though I felt God wanted no part of me. In my state of sadness, nothing I could say could explain how I felt: that my family's love was not enough, and that I had no reason to believe in God, much less live another day. I was convinced that I would die one of the brokenhearted.[3]

E. Lynn tried to commit suicide. Before he did, however, he turned to family members who loved him and cared for him. They included his favorite aunt and her son, who was a minister. They gave him love and support, but this was not enough. His problem was that he thought God cared nothing about him. So he swallowed all the tablets from a full box of sleeping pills. Before he closed his eyes for the last time, he began a conversation with God. He relates:

> I crawled into my bed and decided to give God a final chance to perform one of the miracles I'd heard about in childhood Sunday school classes. I talked silently to God, telling him that I was ready to leave this place called earth. I asked Him to forgive me for taking matters into my own hands, but I knew He would understand my pain and knew my heart. I closed my eyes and believed I was closing them for the last time.[4]

The next day, Harris awoke in his vomit. As soon as he awakened, he knew that God was intimately involved in his life. He also knew he was being given time to get his life together. This new and wonderful knowledge made him want to live. He felt his suicide attempt — and survival — was for a divine reason.

Exploring what lay at the roots of his deep depression, Harris realized he was pervaded with feelings of loneliness and shame. He did not know whether the pain was caused by his being gay or black or both. He knew he felt disconnected from the black community, but he felt proud to be black. And so he decided that perhaps being gay was the source of his problem.

Insight into the life of Harris from a therapeutic standpoint begins with what he has to say about his early life. He grew up in church, and he remembers one Easter when he was to make his Easter speech. He indicated that Easter Sunday was the one day in the year where he could count on his father being in church with his mother. On the Sunday morning before church, he and his sisters showed off their new clothes, hoping for their father's approval. The girls modeled their clothes the way girls do; noticing his father's pleasure, Harris followed their example, thinking that he would likewise win his father's approval. Instead, Harris's behavior disgusted his father, who launched into a series of negative comments about Harris that left the boy stunned. That feeling was exacerbated by his father physically ripping off Harris's coat, which he felt was buttoned like a girl's outfit. Then followed a confrontation between Harris's parents over how he was being babied by his mother.

Harris's memories of how he felt that Easter Sunday stayed with him throughout his adult life: that his father was very disappointed in him, and that he called him a sissy. Though Harris did not know what a sissy was, he decided that day that he would never be one. The messages that Harris received from his father about his worth and value were reinforced by physical violence toward Harris and his mother. His father made him very fearful, and reminded him that he was a poor excuse for a son. Harris understandably felt that his father hated him. He wanted to be a teacher, but his father said only sissy boys wanted to be teachers. He would play school where he was the teacher, and his father would kick all his books and fake report cards off the porch.

Harris writes that his father's beatings made him retreat into a world of silence in which he created a make-believe world that gave him comfort. In his head he created the ideal family. His father's treatment of him made him aware that the real world would never take kindly to "a sissy boy whom even a father couldn't love."[5] He felt that his father had stolen his childhood from him before it even started.

His father recruited Harris into an identity and a story that were not his own creation. His father was laying the foundation for Harris to hate himself; he forced Harris to think that the only way to be accepted was not to be effeminate or a sissy. He was being forced to look at the world from a particular perspective that would alienate him from feeling good about who he was coming to be — indeed, who he actually was.

The conversations that became dominant for him were the ones he heard from his father. The rest of the family loved him and tried to make up for what the father did, but the damage had already been done. Yet fortunately, as an adult, Harris went on a healing pilgrimage that involved certain practices of the self and practices of care that enabled him to significantly edit the story into which he had been recruited by his father.

The Practices of Self Used by E. Lynn Harris

The practices of self make up a political process. Recruiting people into stories and identities that are not their own makes people powerless and disenfranchises them by excluding them from creating their own stories and identities. Editing the identities and stories into which one has been recruited is an important step in recovering one's own agency. The significance of what Harris has to teach us is not in how he was recruited, but how he overcame the internalization of oppression that was the result of that recruitment.

I am a very traditional person when it comes to the gay life and lifestyle. I accept the fact that there are people who desire to be sexually with people of the same sex, but I am much more comfortable when they are celibate. I do feel, however, that God is using some gay people to teach us about God's grace and love, and I feel that E. Lynn Harris is one of these people. In fact, it is Harris's transparent life as a gay person with God that represents the gift that he has to give to all of us. It is his desire to tell of God's love of him and his recovery from abuse that has become his evangelical and political agenda. In my mind, his goal is neither to convince anyone that homosexuality is normal nor to make its acceptance his primary goal. Rather, he tells a story of how God's involvement in his life is bringing healing and wholeness.

I use his memoirs in my course entitled "Inner Healing and Pastoral Care" because his transparency and his ability to let us see God at work in his life is the foundation to becoming a whole person. Transparency in telling his own story is a rare gift, and reflecting on the lessons he has to tell us about the practices of self can contribute to all of our lives.

Though transparency is a practice of self in our contemporary society, it is rooted in Jewish rabbinic tradition, which focuses on the role of clergy in modeling and embodying the values of the faith in ways that transform the lives of others.[6] The practice of transparency has to do with how we treat ourselves, how we treat strangers and our friends, how we speak to God, how we live our personal lives, and what policies we support nationally and locally. Key is the fact that religious people are viewed as vessels and mediators of God's presence, and how we embody God's presence is important in the transformation of the lives of others. Through authentic living we can get a glimpse of God's work in our lives.

Harris's memoir is an attempt to write transparently so that we can see how God has been at work in transforming his life.

His hope is that his self-project will be an example of how God can also work in our lives.

Harris practices privileging conversations with God, which he calls listening to the snow as opposed to the rain. He also uses self-exploration and reflection within the context of therapy, practicing self-awareness through journaling, and the practices of celibacy and sobriety to achieve personal agency.

Though Harris's transparency enables us to envisage God at work in his life bringing transformation, his transparency is not the source of this gift. It is his relationship with God through Jesus Christ that permits him to show his life to the world and to make it a resource on which all of us can draw, regardless of the nature of our own problems.

Not only does he give God the credit for the transformation taking place in his life, he also has learned to privilege or make primary in his life these conversations with God. In fact, his distinction between listening to the snow as opposed to the rain is a way of him telling us how God conversation or listening to God is central for him. For him, rain dreams were the ones that society produced for him, such as the expectation of getting married and having a successful career.[7] His snow dreams are the aspirations, like writing what he listened to inside him without worrying about the expectations of others. In one of his novels, a character describes heaven as a place where one can hear the snow.[8] Harris notes that images of being a writer came to him in images of the snow. He listened to the snow — that is, he was privileging God's voice in his life over all other voices and conversations. This voice led him to share his story in novels first. Later he wrote his memoirs, through which we could really see God at work. Thus, writing about his snow dreams was his way of not only listening to God, but also a way to clarify his role and mission in life. Thus, the practice of writing became a *practice of the self* in the sense that he was discovering his personal mission and purpose in life: to tell his story, and in telling it allowing others to see God at work in it — which then in turn motivated them to make God conversation central in their lives.

The practice of transparency is rooted and grounded in the practices of wisdom received in relationship to God.[9] Wisdom says that conversing with God is for the benefit of the person seeking God, and the benefits growing out of one's relationship with God are personal growth and agency.

Harris's practice of transparency was a political act. Personal agency becomes a political act when one believes that one can change one's own life and have a positive influence on the lives of others. Harris's political agenda is to show that God cares deeply about one's life, including one's sexual orientation, and that one can trust God not to abandon anyone because of his or her sexual orientation.

One of the benefits Harris received from conversation with God was the ability to make significant choices. He testifies that through the power of prayer as well as the practice of attending therapy sessions he learned that he could make choices in his life.[10] He says that he felt God did not change his attraction to men, though he asked God to do this. Rather, what he learned was that he could distinguish between being gay and living the gay lifestyle. Harris even said that he realized that it may have been the *way* he was living his life that was the problem in his life, rather than his sexuality per se.[11]

Harris speaks from a very traditional theological framework in which being gay is alright as long as one is celibate or not practicing homosexuality. The practices of celibacy and how celibacy and being sober added to his healing and transformation helped him to visualize that he could make choices.[12]

Also important in Harris's recovery is the impact that the practices of connecting with others had on his transformation and agency. When he was ashamed of himself, he would withdraw from others, but this would only compound his despair, his drinking, and his self-loathing. Gradually through therapy and much prayer, he was able to allow those who loved him unconditionally to impact his life. He finally came to see that he had more problems with his sexuality than did others who loved him.

Harris also practiced editing the stories into which he was recruited. That is, he identified the dominant conversation that he had internalized from what he had heard in wider culture and decided whether this internalized conversation is growth producing or growth inhibiting. So, aside from his feelings of worthlessness, Harris had also internalized the message that he had to be perfect. This conviction was grounded in the belief that he was worthless and that others would therefore not be interested in him. He felt others could pick up his basic flaw in his personality, and he felt that being perfect would attract people to him.[13] This story too he had to edit in order to thrive.

The practice of editing begins with a realistic exploration of one's internalized convictions. The ability to look at oneself requires the capacity for honest self-reflection. Harris needed help in exploring his convictions, given the nature of his early abuse and his practicing of the gay lifestyle that often exacerbated self-loathing. This kind of help comes from psychotherapy, and Harris spent as many as five days a week in therapy at one period in his move toward healing.

Therapy provides alternative conversations that counter the messages that one has previously internalized. The internalizing process of conversation is very complex, but its basis lies in a relationship where the therapist accepts the counselee unconditionally. Slowly the counselee begins to internalize the positive attitude of the therapist, and this positive attitude becomes the source of one's own feeling good about oneself. At some point in the therapy, the counselee has sufficient strength to begin to explore his or her life and the negative things he or she has internalized from others.

In sum, Harris's memoir chronicles how he moved from self-rejection to self-acceptance. It was a slow process of combining many different practices that together form a whole arsenal. They included the practices of participating in God, the practices of self-reflection, the practices of transparency, the practices of prayer, and several others. Such practices helped him to distinguish between being gay and living a gay lifestyle as well as to risk participating in the lives of others who cared for him. The source of his true feelings of worth and value came from his participation in God's life, and this then became the basis on which he risked engaging life. His memoir is an attempt to let others in on how God has changed his life.

Liberation in the Life of Linda Hollies

Linda Hollies is another person who has discovered her own power and voice and is using it to transform the lives of others. She is a minister in the United Methodist Church, and a prolific writer. What makes her story compelling is that she discovered her sense of personal power and agency as a woman through a variety of practices, particularly those that helped her see beyond God's male gender.

For too long, her image of God was dominated by an internalized image of God shaped by abuse at the hands of her minister father and the complicity of her weak mother. What she learned about God did not help her discover her own personal power because of what she was being taught implicitly and explicitly about God and gender. She only learned about her personal agency through being led by scripture to a woman of personal force in the book of Proverbs in the Old Testament. One could say that she practiced scriptural reading that allowed the text to interpret her.

Hollies found the thirty-first chapter of Proverbs to be an essential step toward her inner healing. In this chapter, she found a woman who gave a prophecy. For her, this was a completely new discovery about her faith and religion, because she had only heard the male voices of scripture up to this discovery. Relating this discovery, she writes:

> A woman of force is one who recognizes and celebrates her personal power. A woman of force is one who is busy working, knowing that she is girded with God's strength and vigor, which allows her to operate with ease and freedom. A woman of force is one who is living the abundant life, not tied to the limitations of her past. A woman of force is full of good works and charity. A woman of force is one who loves and reveres the Lord. A woman of force shall be praised. Her own works and deeds will praise her. She is trustworthy. She is faithful. She is sympathetic. She is intelligent and industrious.[14]

She continues:

> A woman of force is one who has a personal, intimate relationship with God. She relies on God's strength. She relies on God's wisdom. A woman of force is Spirit-filled, Spirit-led and Spirit-controlled. She has the fruit of the Spirit operating and evidenced in her life. She walks tall. She speaks with wisdom and the authority of God. She is a teacher. She is a leader. Other women look up to her. For she is known as a choice jewel among God's resources.[15]

It is clear here that Hollies sees herself as a woman of force, and the scripture interpreting her life at this point was no mere coincidence. Rather, it was the Spirit of God transforming her previous ways of seeing herself and God. It was the power of scripture leading her to where she needed to go in order for her to grow and be transformed.

According to womanist theologian A. Elaine Brown Crawford, transformation takes place in women's lives when their theology and moral judgments mature and develop, and when the circle of influence leading them into abuse begins to reverse itself.[16] The significant point is that the knowledge, insight, and mature growth experienced as the result of encountering God in scripture reverses the way one has been shaped by one's previous experiences and social context. The maturity leads to a reframing and editing of past experiences in ways that produce growth and development.

The concept of woman of force growing out of Hollies's reading of scripture reinforced her ministerial role of helping other women who have been abused to move toward inner healing. She has a calling and mission to empower the lives of other women. Thus, her personal agency led to a political agenda and efficacy.

Scripture reading was not the only practice in which Hollies engaged. The practices of formation in seminary, the practices of self-exploration in Clinical Pastoral Education, and the practices of self-care through personal therapy combined with Bible reading helped her to see herself in a completely different light. The practices of self-exploration include personal awareness of one's own wounds, and the admission that wounds have power over one's life and affect one's behavior.[17] The practices of self-care include sharing the wounds with significant others, confessing the wound and the power it has over one's life, making peace with oneself, and increasing the choices one has for self-exploration.[18] Finally, Bible reading is also a method of self-care in that it orients our wounds toward conversations with God.[19] Over time, these diverse practices helped her to edit her God image, which was preventing her from experiencing the woman of force within herself.

Liberation and Wilson Goode

Wilson Goode was the first African American mayor of Philadelphia. The key to understanding his ascendancy to being mayor is the role that his faith, his local congregation, and his college played in helping him translate his personal agency into political efficacy. One of the hallmarks of the African American church is the connecting of one's faith to a life of service and vocation to the community. One is not expected to be selfish about one's gifts and graces, but rather to use them to benefit the common good. Wilson Goode was in this way a product of the black church and a black college that helped him to connect his personal growth with service to his community.

One of the sad things about some white school systems in the North during the 1950s and 1960s is that many of its white teachers functioned to recruit African American students, especially male, into negative identities that undermined our desire to go to college and to make something of our lives. This was Wilson Goode's experience as well as that of my brother and me. Often it was the white guidance counselor who discouraged black youngsters from going to college, believing that they did not have the family and academic background to pursue college. Many white guidance counselors assumed blacks had inferior backgrounds without even investigating whether it was true or not. For example, my brother and I were told that we were not college material even though our parents were college graduates. In fact, my father had college and seminary degrees, and my mother was a graduate of the University of Pennsylvania, an Ivy League school.

Wilson Goode came north from North Carolina with the dream of going to college. He said he also left the South with resentment toward whites for limiting his parents' aspirations.[20] His parents were sharecroppers, and they were systematically kept in a servile existence through racism. By coming north, Wilson and his parents thought he would overcome the slavelike conditions he was leaving behind. He soon found that the North had its own problems, and it also attempted to recruit him into feelings of inferiority although the racism was less overt than in the South.

Wilson did well in school and had access to integrated schools in Philadelphia. Philadelphia schools had white teachers and black teachers, yet some white guidance counselors

were in strategic positions where they could continue to recruit African American youth into negative identities. Goode
gives a striking example.

> I fought feelings of inferiority when the counselor in my
> Philadelphia high school insisted that I be placed in an in-
> dustrial arts program explaining, "Willie, you're from the
> farm. Therefore, you should know how to work with your
> hands." "And not your mind" was the unspoken message.
>
> Eventually I was placed in an academic program, but
> not before my will was damaged and nearly broken. But
> the God who comes out of nowhere renewed me through
> the faith and support of my church, giving me the courage
> to apply to college and earn enough money to attend
> Morgan State in Baltimore.[21]

The advice of Goode's guidance counselor had a serious
impact on Goode's will. Goode gave up his dream of going to
college, and gained employment at a tobacco company where
the work was more restrictive and lonely than the work back
on the farm. One day at church his pastor's wife pulled him
aside and asked him about his future. Wilson told the pastor's
wife what his guidance counselor said. She then provided what
in pastoral counseling terms is called confrontation. She told
him that it really did not matter what the guidance counselor
had said.[22] Whatever excuse Goode provided, the pastor's wife
countered it. Finally, the pastor's wife told him to save his
money to go to college, and later the church also provided
him with a scholarship. Goode concluded that when the world
told him he could not do something, God provided him with
someone who said he could.

Goode also had a hunger for public service. Morgan State College in Baltimore satisfied that hunger. He said that the hallmark philosophy of this black college was the Promethean Principle, Prometheus being a man who risked his life to bring back fire to humankind. The inspiration of this Greek mythical character encouraged him to make a commitment to public service.[23]

In the Christian formation of many African Americans there is the expectation that one's personal life will eventuate in service to others. It is not enough to develop one's self; it is important to give something back to the community. Christian formation in black churches connects personal agency with political and social efficacy.

The Practices of Participating in God

In the cases of E. Lynn Harris and Linda Hollies, participation in the life of God was critical. A key element in African American pastoral care and counseling is the belief that God is providentially involved in the processes of care and counseling,[24] leading all things toward a positive end. What makes this providential view of God important in some contemporary theology is the way modernity views humans as having lost confidence in God's providential ways. For example, Charles Gerkin points out that many people have lost confidence in the reality of all things working together for the good.[25] Others have pointed out that the Enlightenment has caused people to question whether it is possible to trust God's involvement in the world.[26] In the case of E. Lynn Harris, he put God to the test, and God proved trustworthy. When his suicide failed, he felt sure it was God moving in his life.

Linda Hollies could not trust the male God of her father's denomination. She found, however, that reading about women in the Bible disclosed to her another image of God, which proved to be what she needed to commence revising her self-understanding as a woman. With this new image of God, she began to seek God for her growth and development in agency.

In the case of Wilson Goode, it is not clear about how he understood God being involved in his situation. It is clear, however, that it was the black church functioning as a village that enabled him to edit the story into which he was being created. It was the pastor's wife who stood in the gap between Wilson and God. Wilson also learned from that church that one should translate one's faith into service to others.

The lives of these three important people illustrate how the practices of self led to personal agency. Their lives also demonstrate how certain practices helped them to alter how they had been recruited, and how their personal transformation then led to their commitments to political change.

◆ *Chapter Four* ◆

Practicing Authentic Self-Awareness as Public Theologians

E VERY PARTICULAR historical period and context has its own conversation about what it means to be a self. African American pastoral care and counseling similarly has expectations about what it means to be a self, and by extension, to be a self in ministry. This chapter explores the practices of an African American becoming a self, a pastoral theologian, a public critic, and a social activist. Historically, clergy who have become social activists tend to reflect the conversational environment of evangelical Christianity, where there is a particular kind of expectation of consistency between one's own personal or private life and one's public life.[1] Yet our political climate attempts to separate private religious morality from public participation. Such conflicting expectations present double-binding messages about how one's private and public life are to be connected.

This chapter explores the practices of becoming a self, including having a vital connection between one's private and public life. The work of the novelist Ernest J. Gaines helps to frame this exploration.

The Novel In My Father's House

In his soul-gripping novel *In My Father's House*, Ernest J. Gaines portrays the dilemma that many public theologians face today: how one's private life and public practice of ministry are interrelated. One's private life includes past and present relationships, indiscretions, and personal habits that have the potential of causing embarrassment if known publicly. One's public life has to do with the public face one promotes. Gaines's novel explores what happens to a clergyperson and civil rights leader when his painful past catches up with him and threatens his public witness.

The protagonist, Philip Martin, is a civil rights leader with an apparently impeccable record, who has a genuine Christian conversion experience and becomes a well-respected minister. But things fall apart for Philip Martin when his son from a relationship many years ago shows up where Philip is carrying out his exemplary ministry. His son is an emotional wreck from many years of living life without his father. Many tragic events have taken place in the life of the young man and the family that Philip abandoned many years earlier. The young man wants revenge because of Philip Martin's abandonment of his family and comes to his father's house to commit suicide. The book concludes with the question of what Philip Martin will do about his life as the result of his son's suicide. His brilliant ministerial career is over. His second marriage and family are threatened. More traumatic than anything else, however, is Philip's questioning God about why he has to suffer these things since he had given himself to God more than fifteen years earlier. Philip no longer has answers, and the book ends with Philip Martin not knowing how to reconcile his past with his present life.

For me, this novel addresses various practices of becoming a self that ministers must confront today; for example, is a religious conversion a specific moment in time or is it an ongoing process involving growth and development over time?

To Philip Martin, it was the former. He understood conversion as being justification. Justification is a theological doctrine of being made right by God. In justification one's past sins are forgiven, but one's past sins and their consequences must be confronted. It was obvious that Philip Martin never expected to have to deal with the consequences of his past sins, and so prays, "Why? Why? Is this punishment for my past? Is that why he's here, to remind me? But I asked forgiveness for my past. And you've forgiven me for my past."[2] He feels God is remote from him, that God has become mute in his present situation.

As a Methodist, my understanding of salvation includes the Wesleyan notions of both justification and sanctification. One must not only feel the love of God and know one's past has been forgiven; one must also realize that the consequences of one's sins remain and that one must work to deal with their consequences through the power and grace of the Holy Spirit and personal courage. Therefore, in my mind Gaines's novel pushes us to expand our sometimes narrow understandings of salvation and our related understanding of the practices of becoming a self.

Gaines's novel is an example of how the practices of self-awareness and specifically how one's unresolved private life can derail one's ability to impact the lives of others in positive ways. Gaines's novel further suggests that the practices of becoming a self require time for self-reflection, prayer, and meditation. These meditative practices give the brain space to connect thoughts and feelings in ways that reinforce certain healthy behaviors. Unresolved emotional problems from the past can surface in ways that the brain must be allowed to process and integrate so that the person can reengage life in a positive way. But this demands time, time apart from our work to reflect on problems that surface in our lives, be-cause such problems do indeed have profound consequence for others' lives. Ernest Gaines's novel helps us envisage how self-awareness and the practices of reflection are key to healthy leadership and influencing the lives of others.

The Separation of the Private and Public

How did we get to this place where the public is separated from the private aspects of our lives? Generally this has been attributed to the Enlightenment in general and in particular to René Descartes (1596–1650). At that time the world began to be thought of in terms of material terms alone, and the physical was separated from the spiritual. Thoughts were also separated from feelings. The stage was set, then, for modernity and the splitting of the private from public life.

Contemporary African American and Christian ethicist E. Hammond Oglesby talks about the fact that our being moral agents is not a matter of isolation and compartmentalization. Rather, it is a matter of participation in an inward journey with God as well as participation with others in a faith community. For him God is the spiritual source of ethics by which we live, move, and have our being.[3] God is not only the ultimate moral source for individuals, but also the source of ethics and morals for cultural and moral formation of community. Drawing on Jeremiah's image of the potter and clay, he indicates that God, the Master Potter, forms individuals and faith communities ethically and morally in the potter's house.[4]

Oglesby's participatory ethics counters the Cartesian model of separating life into discrete compartments. Instead of "I

think, therefore, I am," he would say, "I am, because I participate." The ethical person and community say that I (we) am
(are) because I (we) participate in God's life and activity. In
other words, the impetus for our character and life as human
beings comes from the fact that we are holistic beings living in
community. To separate people from such an organic wholeness is to distort reality and make us more vulnerable to the
exigencies of life. To split the private and public aspects of our
lives is to play with self and destroy community.

Indeed, separating the private from the public in our lives
makes us more vulnerable. Oglesby suggests that if we put
more trust in our critical reason (he calls it our secular wisdom)
than in our religious faith, if we distrust our religious faith
orientation, this distrust undermines our ability to envisage
the reality that God is the center of our valuing, our meaning,
and of our human worth.[5]

Garth Kasimu Baker-Fletcher, an African American Christian ethicist, is particularly interested in this connection
between our private and public lives as clergy, and the dan-
gers of severing the connection. He helps us to understand
that making holy ethical choices and living holy lives is not
something we should do apart from the world. Rather, we must
live holy lives in the midst of a world where our ethical and
moral choices are ambiguous at times. He uses the metaphor
of "dirty hands" versus "holy hands" to characterize the moral
choices we make and the consequences that result when we
live in the world. He says:

> The problem of moral ambiguity is peculiarly exacerbated
> for a Christian ethicist because the inner goal of Christian
> spirituality might well be characterized as living a holy

life, raising up "holy hands" because one's heart has been made holy by the cleansing power of the Holy Spirit. In this framework I would characterize Christian ethics as seeking to guide our lives toward the goal of holiness — to lift up holy hands even as we wrestle with the inevitability of getting dirty hands. Existentially and religiously, how do we help each other to grapple with the exalted goals of living into the life of sanctification while finding ways to use our dirty hands with integrity and dignity?[6]

Philip Martin's problems with his past life reflect how vulnerable he had become because he disconnected his past life from his present life. While his life had been transformed by Christian conversion, he did not subject his past life to the transforming power of the gospel. In fact, he psychologically denied his past. But this was not enough to make his past life disappear: it returned with a vengeance, forcing Philip to deal with it. Unfortunately, the novel ends with Philip's life in complete shambles.

Contemporary Connecting Models

There are several contemporary movements that help us envision life as a connecting whole. One such movement is the emotional intelligence movement that I mentioned earlier. There are significant implications from this movement for understanding self-care. Emotional intelligence tells us how the practices of becoming a self connect with political realities.

In the best seller *Primal Leadership: Learning to Lead with Emotional Intelligence*, Daniel Goleman and his colleagues show how the practices of self-awareness lead to social awareness, and how relationship management leads to social management.[7] In other words, the development of self has direct social implications and impacts powerfully the lives of others. The point is that political efficacy begins with believing that one can have a positive impact on the lives of others.

In the model of emotional intelligence, the practices of self-awareness begin with "reading one's own emotions and recognizing their impact."[8] A related skill is accurate self-assessment, which means knowing one's own strengths and limitations. Finally, self-confidence is related to self-awareness, and self-confidence is a good sense of one's own self-worth and capabilities.

Undermining self-awareness is one of the major political strategies of racism. Getting a people to doubt their worth and value as human beings by creating images of worthlessness protects racial position and social status. Thus, enabling African Americans and other socially devalued persons to practice self-awareness is the first step in undercutting the impact of racism.

Self-awareness leads to social awareness and social competence. Awareness of self leads to empathy or the awareness of the emotions of others, understanding their perspectives, and becoming actively interested in others, say Goleman and his colleagues.[9] Self-awareness also leads to structural awareness of organizations in the sense that it becomes possible to discern social currents, decision networks, and politics that impact the lives of others.

Yet the connections between the practices of self-awareness and social awareness must be nurtured and developed intentionally. For example, Philip Martin needed time away from his active civil rights activity in order to do some inner work related to reconciling with his past. As long as he was disconnected and alienated from his past, he was vulnerable to being exploited by the white power structure.

In the novel, his unresolved issues from his past undermined his integrity as a civil rights leader. One of the white power brokers in the community discovered Martin's connection with his long-neglected son from his first marriage, and this power broker used his knowledge to undermine Philip's role in one of the demonstrations his civil rights organization was planning. The power broker locked up his son and only released him when Philip agreed not to lead the civil rights march that had been planned. Had Philip not been so vulnerable because of his past, he would not have been so easily derailed from his civil rights objectives.

The practices of self-awareness should not only include one's present life. The practices of self-awareness need to include one's own past as well. The problems of unresolved past hurts surface at the strangest times. So we do well as pastoral counselors to help leaders focus attention on the relationship between personal and social agency, to reconnect the private and the public, to start attending to what is right before our eyes, before the crisis erupts.

In addition to self-awareness translating into social awareness, self-management translates into relationship management within organizations.[10] Self-management involves controlling one's emotions, being transparent with feelings and emotions, being adaptable to changing situations, being ready to act, and seeing the positive side of things. The consequences of such practices of self-management have a direct impact on one's ability to be an influential leader, to persuade others, to initiate change, to foster the abilities of others, to manage conflict, to cultivate bonding, and to build teamwork and collaboration.[11]

The practices of self-awareness and self-management as proposed in the emotional intelligence movement lay the groundwork for a continued effort to foster a connection between pastoral counseling and the political process. The practices of self-awareness and self-management have social and political consequences.

It is possible to talk about the practices of self-awareness that lead to social involvement. Goleman talks about emotional intelligence because the brain performs multiple functions where people are connected to each other through brain functions. For example there is a brain-to-brain connection through humor. He says:

> Resonance, in terms of brain function, means that people's emotional centers are in synch in a positive way. One of the most powerful and most direct ways to make that resonant brain-to-brain connection . . . is through laughter.[12]

Humor has the capacity to influence the emotional centers of the brains of others so that they are able to move toward positive solutions to problems. Moreover, negative feelings from leaders can hijack others, preventing them from focusing on problems and on solutions.

Philip Martin's preoccupation with unresolved issues from his past life crippled his ability to have a positive impact on those he was leading in the civil rights movement. He was emotionally unavailable to lead people at crucial times in the community's struggle for human and civil rights. There was an emotional disconnection between himself and those he was leading, and the resonance between himself and his people needed for leadership did not exist. As a result, he was immediately voted out of office.

Brain research and its application to leadership and emotional intelligence help us understand better the need to be intentional about taking time out to care for one's unfinished emotional work. Emotionally intelligent people make good leaders because they are free from preoccupations with unresolved personal issues from the past. They are free to invest all of their emotions in those whom they are leading. When the emotional investment is not there for others to draw on, it is hard to lead. Consequently, the connection between one's private and public life is important and essential for leadership.

Separation of Public and Private in Wider Culture

While there are theological and philosophical reasons for keeping the private and public spheres of our lives related, there are some practical reasons for doing so as well. Gabriel Fackre, the Samuel Abbot Professor of Theology Emeritus at Andover Newton Theological School, suggests, "Over time, government — especially democratic government that depends on the confidence of the people in its processes — cannot survive without some measure of trustworthiness in its elected leaders."[13] Embedded in this understanding of government is the conviction that public leadership influences the behavior of persons in our culture. There is no way to escape the interrelationship between what a public leader does in his or her private life and the behavior of others once the leader's private life activities are revealed — both the good and the bad. Pastoral counselors often discover that the revelations of problems that public leaders have in their private lives become the content of their parishioners' counseling sessions.

The issue of public confidence and trust in the elected leaders of the United States and the free world has emerged as a central issue in the aftermath of Bill Clinton's sexual indiscretions with Monica Lewinsky and other women while in positions of public, political authority and power. Prominent sexual abuse scandals in political parties, combined with the Enron scandal and other displays of corporate greed, precipitated the loss of confidence in our stock market; along with the attacks of September 11, 2001, these events have resulted in the entire nation reevaluating its values. We have decided that the character and integrity of our public leadership really matters. It seems that the popularity of George W. Bush early on, when compared to that of Bill Clinton, came from people's confidence in the apparent integrity of the former, although since then, for many people that confidence has been eroded because of Bush's apparently duplicitous reasons for beginning the Iraq war. The shift in the elections in 2000 and 2004 seem to signal, at least for the time being, that the nation is using a different moral barometer in evaluating its leadership. Integrity in leadership is being reevaluated; consistency between one's private and public lives does make a difference.

We can conclude that conversations at the wider cultural level encourage some to practice splitting public and private life in unhealthy ways. Indeed, people are influenced by the conversations taking place at the macro-societal level. African Americans were influenced greatly by President Clinton. Some of us think that his abuse of women was a private matter and did not impact his ability to govern. Yet, it is clear that private conduct does influence the confidence that people have in the leader. In an article I wrote in response to Clinton's problems in the Monica Lewinsky case I addressed the interconnection between the life of Clinton as president and the lives of African Americans. First, African Americans put a lot of trust in a leader who espouses their deeply held values. In fact, Clinton had unprecedented popularity among African Americans because he was able to communicate his care for African Americans and our predicament as human beings in the United States. I tried to explain this remarkable phenomenon as follows:

> My explanation is that the President shares a small-town, folksy, rural style with black preachers and Southern white politicians. Such a style, when used by an attractive, gifted, and charismatic figure, resonates at a deep level with African-American Christians, especially when that figure — notably a preacher/politician — articulates some of the central values to which African-Americans adhere.[14]

Indeed, Clinton was able to address the deep feelings of African Americans by connecting with their souls through the use of key images and metaphors. We actually felt he understood our pain and predicament. We gave him the status of prophet and fighter for our rights — as we often do with those who have great gifts. Moreover, we also treat such persons like star athletes and exempt them from the behavioral expectations and moral requirements that we have for others. We find all kinds of excuses for the lax moral behavior of the empathetically gifted preacher/politician who identifies with our cultural plight. Thus, we held Clinton to a different standard than we did others.

The basic question that I raised about this turning a blind eye to his abuse of women is whether we are better off in the long run without such leaders. Because of their vulnerability and because of our emotional reliance on their leadership, the downfall of such leaders has a tremendously negative impact on our morale. My conclusion is that consistency and congruence between the preacher/politician's private and public life leaves African Americans less emotionally vulnerable:

African-Americans need leaders who do not engage in self-destructive and self-sabotaging behaviors that make them a political liability. If a preacher/politician is known to have personal practices and habits that might hurt him or her and lead to removal from office, we should avoid electing that person to office. It is reasonable to expect that our leaders would have the personal maturity and integrity to behave in ways consistent with their office. Too much is at stake for the preacher/politician to engage in private activities that compromise truth and integrity.[15]

A good life is more than just economic and material well-being; it is also living with honesty, fidelity, compassion, commitment, steadfastness, and consistency that also make life meaningful both for individuals and communities. In short, separating the public and private aspects of our lives distorts the nature of what it means to be a whole person.

The Practices of Self-Recovery

Despite the conflicting messages about the connection between our private and public lives, it is important from a theological anthropology dimension as well as from a secular holistic view of persons to try to keep consistency between one's personal life and one's public life.

In the TV interview with Dan Rather on 60 *Minutes*, former president Clinton talked about the practices of the recovery of self that he used in order to deal with the problems to which his sexual practices led.[16] He indicated that he had had to engage in at least a year of personal, marital, and family counseling. He also indicated that he always had an active prayer and meditative life that supported him in coming to grips with the problems in his personal life.

It is clear to me that it was important for Clinton to appear on TV as well as to publish his book to let the world know about his healing. In my mind, his public airing of his healing is his recognition that one cannot separate one's private and public life when one is an influential leader.

In presenting actual practices of self-recovery, we recall the problems that Phillip Martin faced because he was disconnected from past existence. Though he was disconnected from his past life, he did have an active prayer life and conversational life with God. Moreover, he made efforts to reconnect with his past life. Although his efforts were too late to save his son, these efforts point to possible steps that he needed to repeat in the process of editing the conversations into which he was recruited or which he embraced. For example, he went directly to God in lament over his situation. He complained that he was entitled to God's special treatment, given the fact that he had lived such an exemplary life for a number of years. While he was guilty of believing that his works should have saved his son, he was in direct conversation with God. Such conversation in the form of complaint or lament is an excellent self-care practice. It opens one to God's caring responses, as happened in Job's situation. Job found comfort in the fact that God responded with care to him (Job 38–42). Only conversation with God over a long period could help Philip deal with the depth of despair he felt. While other people are important in this process, the dark night of the soul Philip experienced at that moment of his life had to be addressed directly by God.

Conversational theory evaluates the conversations that a person has internalized and introduces alternative conversations. Phillip Martin internalized a popular biblical and theological theme known as blind triumphalism, referring to the belief that Jesus had already returned a second time, and, therefore, suffering and pain in life were over.[17] His blindness was his inability to face pain and suffering realistically. Theologically, the reality is that healing, peace, and wholeness must be found in the midst of suffering and pain and not in its absence. Thus, a theology that helps people find possibilities for hope and meaning despite the reality of pain and suffering is essential.

Philip Martin's strength was his relationship with God, although he called this into question when he faced the wilderness and Job-like challenges. Clinton's relationship with God was also a critical strength that he employed throughout his presidency. In the practices of self-recovery, one's relationship with God, no matter how strained, is a tremendous resource on which to draw.

Historically, the doctrine that undergirds the practices of self-recovery participating in the life of God is called sapience and results in wisdom that comes from relating to God. The heart of sapiential theology is the conviction that one can trust one's relationship with God to produce positive results, and the results derived from fellowship with God contribute positively to one's development and well-being.[18] Despite the pain and suffering that one may be experiencing currently, sapiential theology encourages people to continue in relationship with God with the Job-like expectation of God's eventual revelation. Philip felt lost and abandoned by God. He thought about turning his back on God and what he had made of his life over the last fifteen years. The novel closes with Philip still in a state of unresolved confusion, not knowing what to do or where to turn.

Second, continuing the practices of self-recovery by relating to God produces positive character traits and personal virtues that are derivative of that relationship. Character and virtue are consequences of being in relationship with God.[19] Philip was in pain, but his relationship with God was a possible valuable asset to him, and the opportunity existed for him to grow in his predicament by continued practicing of self-recovery by participating in God's life.

Closely related to practices of self-recovery are practices that grow out of storying our experiences. We are story-formed people, and we become selves by internalizing certain conversations in which we participate. These conversations provide us clues as to what is important as well as to how to participate and to relate to life as a whole. The facility with which we become whole persons depends on how well we privilege or prioritize certain conversations in our lives.[20] Conversations are the foundations of the stories that shape our lives. Stories compete for priority in our lives, and prioritizing certain stories over other stories is essential to the process of becoming whole.

Philip Martin was not in a bad place in the process of maturing and becoming a whole person. Growth and development in our Christian lives come as a result of our readiness to take the next step in the maturational process. He had been engaging in practices of improving himself through relating to God through daily conversations with God and living a virtuous life, yet living his life introduced challenges that forced him to face a part of his life on which he had turned his back. He had cut himself off from his past and its related stories. Psychologically and spiritually, he could not move to the next stage of growth without facing these: they would always remain a hidden force threatening to undo his present life and development.

How Philip sought to reengage his past life and its related stories was psychologically significant and spiritually appropriate. He did so chiefly by remembering — that practice in which one reenters the former relational environments and stories that shaped one's original conversations.[21] In many cases this involves reengaging one's family of origin or one's family of creation (e.g., family through marriage). Within these families of creation are conversations that give meaning to our lives. If our family of creation dissolves, one must review at some point the impact of the dissolution of the marital or close family relationship on the conversations that have shaped one's life if one is to continue to grow. To neglect this review is to postpone inevitable pitfalls and problems.

When Philip Martin's son resurfaced in his life, Philip suddenly and appropriately set aside his work and relationships in order to attend to unfinished relational and story work. What was inappropriate was the fact that he gave no warning to others and made no preparation for reentering his old world. Rather, he abruptly left his work responsibilities and his current family to attend to the past. He returned to his former community, and he began to reengage people who could help him piece together the story that led up to his son's suicide and find out what happened to his first wife and the rest of his children. What he discovered was very painful and overwhelming for him. It was hard for him to integrate the losses that occurred as a result of his being a deadbeat father and unfaithful husband.

The novel ends before the remembering process could be completed. At some point in the remembering process Philip would have had to review consciously the conversations and stories that shaped his life with his first family. He would have to own his role in the destruction of that first family, and to find a way to accept his responsibility in its demise. He would have to face the fact that he had a significant role to play in his son's suicide as well.

This review of one's past life and the role one played in creating it is called externalization or the process of self-care, where one reflects through introspection and self-examination on experiences that shaped one's life.[22] Externalization is a practice of self-recovery; it is a process of consciously reviewing conversations and stories that have been internalized for the purposes of editing, updating, revising, deconstructing, or re-authoring them. Deconstructing and re-storying are similar to externalization, and they can be used interchangeably.

The purpose of engaging in the practices of re-storying, re-membering, deconstructing, and editing is to increase personal agency. In Philip Martin's case this would have meant increasing his ability to participate more fully in shaping the conversations and stories that formed his life. Re-storying would have made him proactive in creating his own story rather than reactive by being recruited into conversations and stories that were not his own.

I have no doubt that Philip was recruited into conversations and stories in his first marriage that were not entirely his own choices. I am sure he was going along to get along, doing the best he could with what he had. Nonetheless, he was accountable for the story he internalized, and returning to this story and reediting it would have led to his further growth and development and agency.

Philip was at a very painful place in his life, but his situation was an opportunity as much as it was a danger. He had an opportunity to re-story his life in ways that would have improved his agency and helped him to reengage life in meaningful ways. The practice of self-recovery through relating to God as he continued to do, along with the other practices of remembering and re-storying, were major resources on which he needed to draw in order to resolve his current crisis.

Attending to the practices of self-recovery through intentionally taking time out increases the personal agency of leaders. When personal agency is increased, such agency becomes a resource for public leadership. In this sense, political efficacy is about enabling others to participate fully in life.

◆ *Chapter Five* ◆

Pastoral Counseling
and Critique of Modernity:
The Practice of Contextual Self-Awareness

ODERNITY SHAPES the conversations that impact the lives of counselees and parishioners we encounter in pastoral care and counseling. Modernity here refers particularly to those dominant conversations characterizing our lives as a free-enterprise country seeking to fulfill its economic goals. Market-driven and commodity images of human worth are the dominant forces impacting our lives. These market-driven images of self-worth are often internalized at the expense of other conversations. The role of pastoral counseling and psychotherapy is to help people become aware of how these market-driven and commodity-oriented images of self-worth impact their lives and to help them find alternative and more growth-facilitating images of their worth. This process is called contextual self-awareness. The pastoral caregiver, also drawing on faith perspectives about human worth and experiences in pastoral counseling and psychotherapy, promotes non-commodity-oriented images of human worth and fosters alternative conversations in public debate as a result of this contextual self-awareness.

Contemporary African American novels illustrate the way that themes of commodification impact the lives of African

Americans today. The "soul" or priorities of any culture can be discerned by examining its contemporary literature. The most prominent cultural conversations shape the basic attitudes, convictions, and beliefs that lie at the basis of human behavior. An analysis of novels in particular can reveal these conversations. The 2002 novel entitled *The Emperor of Ocean Park* by Stephen Carter is illustrative.[1]

Stephen L. Carter's Novel

The Emperor of Ocean Park reveals the appropriate role of pastoral care and counseling in helping a prominent African American lawyer to edit internalized cultural conversations that have impacted his midlife crisis. He was questioning whether the way he had lived and was living his life was meaningful anymore. By societal standards he had achieved a lot in terms of professional advancement and wealth, but midlife precipitated his concern about how he was participating in life and whether there was more to life than what he had accumulated.

The novel takes place in New England and is about a prominent African American former judge who was nominated to the U.S. Supreme Court by Ronald Reagan, but who suddenly withdrew from the nomination in disgrace because of the appearance of corruption. As the story unfolds, a complicated plot emerges in which the son, a middle-aged law professor at Yale University, is challenged by a note left behind by his deceased father to pursue his untimely and mysterious death. The reader delves into the unfolding drama of the story hoping to find out that the dead judge is exonerated from the insinuated corruption and hoping to be assured of his utter integrity. This does not happen, however. As Talcott Garland, the lawyer son of the judge, delves deeper into the mysterious death of his father, he discovers a story of intrigue and corruption at the highest level of the Supreme Court, namely, that his father had a man murdered to avenge the death of his daughter, who was killed in a hit-and-run car accident. No one pursued the case of the hit-and-run because the perpetrator was the son of a very high government official. So Judge Oliver Garland took matters into his own hands.

There are many plot twists and turns as Talcott attempts to unlock the puzzle and codes left behind by his father to find out the truth. Talcott and his friends and colleagues are often in danger as he gets closer to the truth. In fact, he almost loses his life when he finally discovers that his own father and one of the most respected sitting judges on the Supreme Court were involved in receiving kickbacks from corporations on cases over which they had presided in their courts.

From the perspective of pastoral counseling, the story is about a middle-aged son who resolves his midlife crisis by no longer idealizing his father as mentor, which he had had to do in order to achieve an important place in society. He had to find a more enduring source of his identity than his father. His midlife task was to make the transition from being a disciple of his father to being a mentor himself. He was at a maturation point where he could face the truth about his father. The theological question that the book raises is: what will be the source of one's new identity when one must face the truth about one's parents and when the human foundations of identity are no longer adequate?

Talcott has learned to negotiate the professional world and the world of family life chiefly through conversations he learned from his parents, particularly his father. Since his father was his ideal, he saw no need to question or be critical of the conversations he was learning and internalizing, and upon which he was patterning his life and career. His father's life became his wisdom guide and filter for what it meant to engage life at its fullest.

Talcott was able to transcend racism and to achieve marked success. He found cultural avenues for the complete expression of his self-understanding, his personal gifts, and his full capacities. He learned to play the cultural game of inclusion very well; therefore, his access to total participation in the U.S. system was assured. If he faced any overt racism and opposition to his abilities to participate in life, he apparently was able to overcome them. Obviously, he had internalized well the conversations that enabled his father to achieve the almost unachievable — an appointment to the United States Supreme Court. Whether Talcott was a token or not, he achieved a great deal and followed the prescribed pattern held out for professional success by wider culture.

The novel is about the unraveling of the "picture perfect" perspective on the world that led to Talcott's success as a prominent lawyer and professor at Yale University Law School. It describes the falling apart of the dominant conversation that enabled Talcott to achieve the success he had as a black man living in a white world. It is about the fallacy of over-internalizing cultural achievement aspirations to the exclusion of many other important values, particularly spiritual values. Talcott had developed a tragically strong allegiance to wider cultural images of prestige, honor, success, and wealth to the extent that he ignored the tragic human flaws existing in all persons regardless of race. He discovered that his father's tragic flaw undermined his father's aspiration to be seated on the Supreme Court, and that his father's life had been more corrupt then he could ever imagine. It was his father's corrupt work and tragic flaw that propelled Talcott to revise the conversations that he had internalized and to pay more attention to the spiritual dimensions undergirding his own life.

This novel shows that the ultimate purpose in life is not to reach the highest office held out by society or to be an exceptional black person, a shining example for other African Americans. Rather, Carter reminds the reader that spiritual conversations with the Source of our existence cannot be excluded from what we internalize, nor can spirit-shaping conversations. Achieving high societal expectations becomes meaningless without a vital spiritual connection that transcends cultural conversations.

The novel, then, is about how Talcott drew on his pastor as well as other relationships to revise, edit, and ground his worldview in a more lasting perspective on life. Talcott had many conversations with one particular pastor, who was vital in his editing of his personal convictions and beliefs. It is from this pastor's modeling that I have gleaned some insight into how internalized conversations can be edited, even well into midlife.

In the process of discovering the truth about his father, one of Talcott's mentors at Yale died. Talcott was asked to say some kind words about his friend and mentor from the law school, and while he was offering his reflections, he began to cry — so much so that he was not able to finish his comments. About the incident he said: "I suppose people think I was crying over Theo. Maybe I was, a little. But mainly, I was crying over all the good things that will never be again, and the way the Lord, when you least expect it, forces you to grow up."[2]

From this admission, we learn several things about Talcott: First, he recognized that one's mentors and parents have clay feet and die. Second, growing up is about giving up illusions and convictions about life and what one will actually achieve. Third, one has to find a more enduring source of one's life once disillusionment sets in about the underpinnings of one's existence. Fourth, one must come to grips with one's own frailty and that of others. And fifth and finally, one must find and build another foundation for one's life that transcends our human foundations.

These five points are supported by another admission by Talcott at the end of the novel when all the truth has finally surfaced, in which he acknowledges his limitations as well as the role of faith in discovering the nature of truth. This passage aptly summarizes that point of the novel:

> I have long been comfortable living without perfect knowledge. Semiotics has taught me to live with ambiguity in my work; Kimmer has taught me to live with ambiguity in my home; and Morris Young is teaching me to live with ambiguity in my faith. That truth, even moral truth, exists I have no doubt, for I am no relativist; but we weak, fallen humans will never perceive it except imperfectly, a faintly glowing presence toward which we creep through the mists of reason, tradition, and faith.[3]

Talcott makes several theological statements about his midlife crisis. The first is that he sees human beings as limited and unable to grasp truth as a whole. (In fact, he uses the theological term "fallen" to describe human's state.) Moreover, he

says that work, family life, and religious life are full of ambi-
guity. Finally, he says that truth is a presence toward which
we move using reason, tradition, and faith. It sounds to me
as if Talcott found the enduring source of his remaining years
on earth, and that that source was a faith which trusted the
unfolding of truth that would be revealed as one engaged life.

Contextual Self-Awareness and Criticism of Modernity

With Talcott in mind, we can say that as critics of cultural conversations, pastoral caregivers introduce alternative images of
human worth and value so that counselees and parishioners
begin to revise the negative ways that cultural conversations
have impacted their lives. With regard to being a cultural
critic, it is important for the pastoral caregiver to constantly
make the connection between the behavior of individuals and
wider cultural conversations. The essential nature of the work
of the pastoral caregiver involves two movements. The first is
to help the counselee and parishioner to identify how wider
cultural conversations impact individual behavior, and the second is to edit these conversations in ways that increase one's
personal agency.

African American literature has been very helpful to me in
identifying cultural conversations, and it can be used in the
work of the pastoral caregivers. *The Emperor of Ocean Park*
reveals important lessons about modernity and the impact it
has on the lives of counselees and parishioners.

The first lesson deals with cultural self-awareness. Talcott
learns the limitations not only of his father's way of achieving
success, but also how to reorient his life to more lasting and
enduring values. For example, he learned that the practices of

civility used by his father were limited. The practices of civility represent the striving of African Americans to achieve access to the social rewards and benefits of larger culture through certain strategies.[4] The strategies undergirding the practices of civility include loyalty to wider cultural values and pursuing what culture holds to be significant, such as wealth, status, position, prestige, and power. It is clear that such values were significant to Talcott's father, but these values are no longer helpful to Talcott as he approaches midlife. Talcott's discovery of his father's frailness and limitations serves as a catalyst for his becoming culturally self-aware. His pastor is also helpful in being a dialogue partner for Talcott as he learns the limitations of what he had internalized from his parents. It takes time for Talcott to realize how limited his father's worldview was, and he needs the help of key people in his life to figure things out. His pastor is one such sounding board for him as he edits and re-authors what he has learned from his father.

The basis of Talcott's cultural self-awareness is what Cornel West calls the "nihilism of the unprincipled use of power." For West, this form of nihilism is the drive to succeed at all costs regardless of the moral boundaries limiting certain pursuits.[5] The practices of decency and integrity are thrown out the window. Talcott's father became a victim of the unprincipled will to power, and he was destroyed in the process. Talcott understands that he cannot live his life following his father's example. Thus, he begins to question what he learned from his father. He begins his search for more enduring values and practices.

It is clear that the works of Stephen Carter represent his own quest for cultural self-awareness. His desire to develop personal integrity and to be a complete and whole person with a congruent private and public life are examples of how the quest for cultural self-awareness is manifested in his life. His criticism of the culture of disbelief is also his attempt to ground his life in spiritual values and part of his quest for cultural self-awareness. He demonstrates that he is very discerning about the kinds of cultural conversations that he wishes to internalize.

His writings are also his way of making his critique of modernity part of the public debate. He makes sure that his cultural self-awareness is translated into political action, by writing nonfiction books about the limitations of the culture of modernity. His novel represents his way of illustrating how people can get caught in the destructive clutches of modernity, and in it he shows how we can escape the bondage of modernity through questioning the values of the pursuit of success, civility, and nihilistic abuse of power.

The Use of Literature in Understanding Modernity

One way to discern quickly the interrelationship of individuals and wider culture is attending to contemporary novels and the kinds of wider cultural conversations they reveal. Carrie Doehring's work in *Taking Care: Monitoring Power Dynamics and Relational Boundaries in Pastoral Care and Counseling* lifts up some important insights about how literature reveals cultural conversations and questions.[6] For example, she points out that selected novels pick up the themes of postmodernity and how culture fosters disengagement from others and merger with one's fantasies — which in turn produces persons who seek power over others as well as opportunities to actualize their fantasies. More precisely, our market-driven culture fosters our disengagement from communal relationships so that we can pursue material wealth. However, our need for relationships with others does not disappear at all; instead, in our computer and electronic age we use fantasies to replace significant relationships. For example, sex is a major vehicle of modern fantasy life, and casual and uncommitted sex serves as a substitute for committed relationships in our culture. In Doehring's mind, disengaged relationships and merger with fantasy life leave people vulnerable to violence.

Doehring shows how novels reveal cultural conversations and how they impact individuals. Novels reveal the level of fragmentation existing in people's lives and relationships as well as how they turn to escapes — such as constructing fantasy worlds — to isolate themselves from the pain of lost relationships. Therefore, one major conversation of contemporary culture says that pain and suffering are unreal and that we should be able to live without them. Therefore, novels reveal how we construct worlds that protect us from seeing and experiencing pain. Novels also do the opposite as well; they show how the worlds we create to escape the reality of suffering are deconstructed.

My contention is that some African American authors have become cultural critics as well as spiritual guides for a culture that appears to be bereft of spiritual values and norms. This is particularly the case with Stephen L. Carter. *The Emperor of Ocean Park* is Carter's attempt to show how Talcott faced the real world to avoid becoming disengaged and to escape the threat of the nihilistic abuse of power which is often symptomatic of people who are disengaged from significant relationships and who use power as a way to substitute for meaningful relationships.

Some people turn to addictive forms of sex to avoid the pain of living without significant relationships. Even though Talcott had a painful marital relationship, he did not turn to sex as a substitute for real interpersonal relationships. He was not going to get caught up in an imaginary world to substitute for his marital failings. What he did was to turn to generative values by investing his time in his young son, who had some real emotional challenges. He began to invest his time in the next generation, making sure that the cycle of the nihilistic abuse of power was arrested in his generation. There would be no negative generational legacy established.

Implications of Carter's Novel
for Pastoral Care and Counseling

Carter as an academic writer and as a novelist is the consummate public critic. The midlife crisis theme of the novel helps us to discern how cultural beliefs, conversations, and practices impact the resolution of the midlife crisis. Carter's novel and his nonfiction publications are his quest to resolve his own midlife crisis. It is my opinion that this novel is the actual resolution of this personal struggle, and he is presenting his resolve for all of us to use in whatever way we choose. As pastoral caregivers we can learn a lot about our task of helping people to edit those internalized conversations that hinder our ability to be full participants in life.

Carter's critique of modernity is that public conversation disallows religious commitment. In fact, he says that deep religious convictions are deemed irrational by the press and popular public conversation. This is his major point in *Culture of Disbelief: How American Law and Politics Trivialize Religious Devotion.*[7] For him, religious devotion refers to religious and spiritual convictions, practices, and attitudes. He recognizes how religious devotions are devalued in the name of rationality, and how they are being devalued not because of secularization, but because religion is viewed as a tool of the religious right.[8] In fact, trivialization means treating religion as an unimportant dimension of the human personality that can be easily discarded. He points out that faith and reason are not incompatible. He declares that he is a Christian . . . "who relies on discernment of the will of God as the path to moral knowledge, and I consider this process no less rational than any of the more secularized forms of moral reasoning that dominate our media and the academy."[9]

His major critique of American culture is that religion is viewed by wider culture as a passing belief and a fad rather than as a foundation on which humans build their lives.[10] In fact, public conversations see religious devotion as peripheral rather than central to what transpires in life. He talks about a trivializing rhetoric, which says, "Do whatever you want to do religiously, but do not take it too seriously." This is the attitude that not only the media takes toward religion; it is also the attitude of political society. His goal is to make a case for people to take the religious seriously as basic to human existence.

Carter's conclusion about the way society treats religious devotion is a key factor to be considered in our attempt to explore the political dimensions of African American pastoral care and counseling. It is very clear that people internalize wider cultural devaluation of religion, and this has a real impact on how they live their lives. For example, counselees often ignore deep religious promptings from within. During an illness, a counselee of mine had a very significant visitation from God, which she completely ignored. When I called this to her attention, she seemed surprised that this was important at all. My response was that the event was significant and represented a turning point in her recovery from depression. Because I valued this event and saw it as significant, she also took the event seriously and began to draw on it as she progressed in her therapy.

African American pastoral care and counseling have made a significant place for spiritual, religious, and theological conversations in its practices. For example, the book *Soul Theology* addresses theological themes that often appear in the counseling sessions of African American counselees.[11] In a real way, African American pastoral care and counseling is a critique of modernity in its practices because of its embrace of faith dimensions. Carter's critique of the culture of disbelief is pivotal to a society that continues to separate faith and values, and African American pastoral care and counseling embrace this critique implicitly.

There is some similarity between the work of Stephen L. Carter and what is being undertaken in pastoral public theology. This includes a critique of the culture of disbelief as well as the effort to introduce faith orientations into public debates. One question remains, however: how does Carter's novel enable us to address the concern of editing conversations that we have internalized that undermine our efforts to be full participants in society based on our full capabilities?

The analysis of the midlife crisis of Talcott and its resolution is instructive.

The Practices of Self-Awareness

From a pastoral care perspective, cultural supports at each stage of the life cycle are critical, particularly at the adult stages of the life cycle. The difficulty with our market-driven society and cultural trivialization of religion and belief is that it offers very little support for resolving the midlife cycle crises. For example, one of the major tasks for resolving the male midlife crisis is to find a more secure basis of one's identity, which is able to transcend cultural expectations. Our market-driven culture forces us to focus on our youthful qualities and capacities while, at midlife, we need to attend to more pressing maturational issues.

The tasks of midlife involve certain key emotional, development, and spiritual dimensions. For men, there are a series of reversals identified by Daniel Levinson.[12] One such reversal is for those in midlife to devote their lives to the pursuit of purposive and meaningful goals that transcend the pursuit of fortune and fame of the youth-oriented culture. Thus, service to others and making a contribution to the next generation seems to be a must for men who are handling appropriately the midlife crises. While Levinson's conclusions relate primarily to white men, white women and African American men follow similar developmental paths if they enter into professional life and the workforce immediately following high school or college. Yet the push and pull of our market-driven culture does not easily support the development of our inner and spiritual lives. Indeed, the development of our inner and spiritual lives is an absolute necessity in midlife if we are to negotiate it. In midlife our youth has declined, our dreams of success have to be modified, and we need to prepare for the remaining days of our lives facing the inevitability of physical decline and death. Spirituality becomes a number-one priority in midlife.

More can be said about developing our inner lives as an important way to negotiate midlife. Midlife requires a looking inward much in the same way that Talcott did in being the vehicle that Stephen Carter used to tell the story of the conflicted character of the judge. Talcott had to look inward rather than outward to find whatever resources he needed to face the truth of his father's life as well as the truth of his own life. His self-image could no longer be based on market-driven success. Rather, it had to be rooted in inner goals and purposes that can only be attended to when the supports of the past have been challenged and shaken by life circumstances and happenstance. Talcott had to develop his faith in something beyond and outside of himself. He could no longer depend on the image and reputation of his pre-midlife dependence on his father.

Talcott also had to learn to transcend his disappointment in others as well as his disappointment in his father. His wife lost interest in him and got involved with one of his students. The book showed how he was able to face this reality and move on with insight, wisdom, and hope. He also had to overcome the loss of his first minister, who was trapped by life and its addictions, and had to learn to live without the support of many of his colleagues, who were very competitive.

Not only did Talcott respond well to the many challenges he faced, while he lost some relationships, he was able to negotiate others. He was able to develop his nurturing side as he cared for his youthful son, who needed him more and more. Midlife seemed to produce for him great satisfaction through his adopting a caring parental role. He also developed new friends as well as the capacity to pick those friends who were able to give as well as to take. The key to all of this was that he developed a relationship with a pastor who helped significantly to navigate the deep waters associated with midlife.

From the vantage point of making a contribution to the critique of modernity, the novel reminds wider society that religious faith is a very necessary part of our developmental lives. Religious faith plays a vital role at every stage of the life cycle, and people need the public sanction of culture to employ their faith in resolving personal issues and concerns. Religion and faith cannot be ignored or excluded from public debate without it having a deleterious impact on our personal lives. Public dismissal of faith and religion will impact pejoratively both the young and old alike.

In the novel, we also see Talcott newly enabled to edit what he had internalized about the meaning of success as a black man in a world dominated by whiteness and its constructs of "success." The concern in the remaining pages of this chapter is to explore the implications of this particular novel for editing internalized themes related to modernity, among them the importance of developing a relationship with God, how such a relationship develops personal virtue and agency, the significance of engaging the appropriate life cycle tasks, and learning to reflect theologically on one's experience.

In one of his reflections, Talcott speaks of relating to God. He turns to his pastor for help in dealing with the many losses that he has encountered in midlife, including the loss of his marriage and the loss of his ideal image of his father. He comments that God forces one to grow up when one least expects it. Talcott believed that God was involved in the maturing process or formation process of his life. Moreover, he felt that God systematically undermined the security that he had in his fantasy world. That is to say, God forced him to have to face the reality of living without the security of his past solutions to problems and his trust in his professional achievements. He had to experience what his father had done in order to begin the revision and editing of what had become an inadequate orientation to his life. His midlife crisis forced him to revise the way he approached his life and profession.

The novel assumes that life itself is the teacher, and that pastoral care and counseling must be ready to assist this inherent life process when it is occurring. Therefore, the role of the pastoral caregiver is to be present for the one in crisis when he or she discovers that past solutions to problems and internalized conversations are inadequate and there need to be new orientations to life. The many conversations that Talcott had with his pastor helped him to revise the old ways he looked at life.

In midlife, one can no longer avoid the reality of suffering. The wider cultural conversation that life should be lived without pain can no longer be avoided. Counselees often bring with them suspicions that the losses and pain they have sustained in life are the way things really are. Therefore, they are in the process of reorganizing their lives and editing their conversations in ways that acknowledge this reality. Our task as pastoral caregivers is to affirm the limitations of their previous orientation to life and acknowledge the need for a transition to a new orientation, as well as to help them to find out how God is leading them through this process.

In the novel God forces Talcott to face reality. As readers, we cannot escape the fact that we are also drawn into the plot of the novel and through it begin to explore and examine our own inability to face reality. The novel gets us to consider what is happening in our lives and how can we change in ways that will lead to more fulfillment. *The Emperor of Ocean Park* enables us to face the necessity of life transition and engaging in the age-specific tasks related to resolving life crises. One literary function of this novel is to assist the reader in engaging appropriately his or her life cycle crisis.

In American Western culture, the dominant cultural conversation about midlife focuses on how to give up one's youthful ambitions and aspirations and settle for not realizing some of our dreams. We also learn to recognize our own shortcomings as well as those of our mentors. We learn to develop our spiritual lives, knowing that our youthful orientation for life can no longer sustain us in the midst of anticipated losses in our physical and relational lives. In essence, we have to wake up and face a reality that we have never dared to encounter.

The novel wakes us up to the reality that life is a series of transitions with age-related cultural conversations to engage. The same is true for the function of pastoral care and counseling. Consequently, pastoral caregivers need to engage the dominant cultural conversations influencing counselees at specific stages of the life cycle and help them to evaluate the conversations in light of (1) the conversations that were inherited from our early upbringing, and (2) the conversations that we, the counselees, are having with God. We hope that the end result is the ability to engage in an appropriate response to the reality of the specific stage of the life cycle in which we find ourselves.

As a pastoral caregiver, I have been influenced by the depth psychological view that the quality of life is enhanced by being aware of and reflecting on the growth processes taking place within oneself. Second, the theological principle of allowing oneself to be shaped by one's relationship with God also requires a level of reflection. Thus, reflection is assumed to be basic to the growth process psychologically and theologically.

Stephen Carter helps us to envisage one of the ends of reflecting on one's life in light of one's relationship with God. Reflection not only draws on the behavioral sciences to gain some perspective on where we are in the life cycle. Yes, recognizing where one is in the life cycle is essential, but Carter helps us to take reflection even further by reflecting on what God is doing in one's life — or, in the case of the novel, Talcott's.

First, God is deconstructing the world that Talcott had constructed. Talcott is being called to mourn and give up a world of innocence in which his father is the center of his life. Now, God is helping him to discover the true center of his life. Most of us draw upon our significant others to help us through the early stages of our existence, but there comes a time when we have to let this world go and trust the leadership of our lives completely to God. The old, idolatrous creations will not be adequate for facing the later stages of our lives. The idea that God is a jealous God and will destroy all gods becomes a reality for Talcott. God forces Talcott to grow up, and growing up means that one has to put one's trust completely in God in order for life to have significant meaning.

Not only is Talcott forced to reflect on the limitations of his previous worldview for making sense in his life. He has to engage in the practice of cultural self-awareness. He is also forced to draw some conclusions about human nature. Not only does God call us to live without our human idols, we are also challenged to face the truth about our existence. Talcott says that we not only have imperfect knowledge, we also perceive truth imperfectly when it is revealed. Talcott states that we come to truth not only by perceiving it imperfectly, but by moving slowly toward its glowing presence using our reason, our tradition, and our faith. Discernment is a slow process in which reason, reflection on tradition, and trusting our relationship with God all combine to lead us toward understanding.

Carter's *Emperor of Ocean Park* enables us to visualize the entire process of how to edit internalized cultural conversations that impact our lives. Talcott's intellectual and emotional commitment to his professional orientation to life became inadequate, and was preventing him from the kind of participation in life that would increase his personal agency. We bring the lives we have constructed into critical engagement with the transitions we are undergoing in our life cycle. We go through a period of deconstruction where we discover that our constructions are no longer adequate for the life we are currently living. We also engage the cultural conversations taking place that impact us as well. We begin to mourn the loss of the old constructions as we give them up. We become realistic about our lives and their limitations, and finally we begin to trust God as we move toward transformation and an orientation to life characterized by trusting in God. As a result, we have added personal agency, and this agency can be used in a variety of ways to participate more fully in life as well as to help others to do the same thing.

So Carter's resolution of his personal midlife crisis and his editing of his internalized conversations have resulted in his resolve to be a public critic of modernity. He warns African Americans and others not to get overly involved in the pursuit of middle-class, professional achievement to the neglect of spiritual and relational values. The seduction of market-driven and commodified images of success have their limitations and cannot provide what we ultimately need. Spirituality and faith, however, are what provide us with what is meaningful, and they facilitate full involvement in life for ourselves as well as for others. Pastoral care and counseling play a significant role in helping us to reorient our lives spiritually and religiously so that our participation in life and in the lives of others becomes more meaningful.

Chapter Six

Challenging Modernity:
Pastoral Care and Counseling
as Public Theology

P ASTORAL CARE AND COUNSELING as political processes not only challenge modernity, they also bring the insights learned from the practice of pastoral counseling to public debate. In developing the role of pastoral care and counseling in public theology, it is important to (1) explore contemporary aggressive secularism, (2) understand the pastoral caregiver as public theologian, (3) understand African American pastoral care and counseling as public theology, and (4) publicly critique the dominant cultural conversation known as nihilism. Pastoral counseling caregivers as public theologians need to address those public debates that focus on sustaining the dignity and worth of human beings. It is important to release the gifts of personal agency within people; it is equally important to address those forces in culture that recruit persons into negative stories, plots, and images that destroy personal agency and full participation in society.

Nat King Cole died in 1964. Four or five years later I learned through one of my white female counselees that race, sex, and religion were integrally connected in the minds of many people. My counselee had been diagnosed from a dynamic personality perspective as a person with a conversion reaction.

A conversion reaction is an ego defense where the person's inner psychological dynamics are projected onto a part of the body, and the purpose of this maneuver is to protect the person's awareness from being overwhelmed by anxiety. During the 1960s in the United States the subject of sex, in particular of white women being attracted to black men, were issues that provoked a great deal of anxiety and fear. My white female counselee had internalized society's anxiety and fear about sex and race, and her psychological defenses against such anxiety began to function. Her executive dimension of her personality, known as the ego, began to convert the anxiety about sex and race to one of her eyes. As a result, she was blind in one eye, but there was no real physical basis for the blindness. Her blindness was symbolic, and blindness was a symptom of her ego's converting her anxiety about both sex and race. Psychologically, her blindness was about her punishment for having what wider society would have deemed taboo thoughts and feelings.

Prior to the death of Nat King Cole, her denying of her sexual feelings was very apparent. Many years after the death of Cole she began to talk about how she felt about him being a TV star and how much she admired him. Eventually, she allowed herself to reveal that she was attracted to him, but she exhibited a great deal of guilt after saying how she really felt about him. The Victorian views about sexual feeling dominated wider cultural conversations in the 1960s; sexual conversations between women and men were deemed inappropriate, and sexual feelings toward a black man had to remain secret. The racist social climate was not ready to deal with white women and black men and romantic relationships between them. Our pastoral counseling relationship, however, became a safe place where she felt comfortable in discussing what she deemed forbidden thoughts and feelings. Eventually, she was able to talk about her positive feelings toward me, also a black man, because of the kind of relationship we had developed in our counseling.

My counselee spent several months trying to talk about sex and race before she was able to do so. She had been recruited by wider culture into specific attitudes toward sex and race: specifically, the expectation that would deny any interest in sex and most particularly any feelings of tenderness toward a black man. Religion helped to do some of the recruiting into denying sexual and racial taboo subject matters. Religion functioned to sanction what were legitimate conversations for people to have. Sex, race, and religion are clearly topics that were forbidden for women, and such recruiting led to many problems of sexual repression and denial of positive feelings related to people outside one's own race.

As I reflect on this counselee of many years ago, it is clear that wider cultural attitudes about sex and race become the stuff that gets internalized by counselees, and such internalizations do eventuate in psychological and emotional problems that call for therapeutic intervention. As a pastoral counselor, my role was to help her explore the internalized cultural prohibitions about sex and race, but it was also to address the wider cultural oppressive attitudes about sex and race. The pastoral counselor's task is to become a public critic of those cultural values that prevent healthy attitudes toward both race and sex. More than this, the pastoral counselor also needs to show how religion mediates wider cultural values.

The role of religion in excluding feelings about sex and feelings of warmth of my white female counselee was extremely important. The connection between sex and race on the one hand, and what some religion teaches about sex is hard to deny, on the other hand. Trying to separate religion and spirituality from sex and race is an impossible task. Consequently, the pastoral caregiver must always keep in his or her awareness the interconnection between race and sex.

While sex and religion are interconnected, the influence of religion on sex does not have to be negative. In fact, a lot of what is taught about sex in religion is extremely helpful. For example, religion always provides a context and boundaries in which genital sex can be practiced. Religion also teaches that sex and sexuality are natural gifts of God's creation. Third, sex and its related practices can serve communal building dimensions through the influence of religion, and religion can serve to control the use of sex for destructive and evil purposes. What is central here is that it is impossible to exclude the role of religion in our understanding of sexuality.

Aggressive Secularism

Just as race, sex, and religion are integrally connected, the place of religion in causing as well as solving many problems must not be overlooked, yet there is a strong effort to keep religion out of public life. Pastoral counselors as public theologians seek to keep the positive and healing role of religion in public debates and to resist any efforts to marginalize religion.

Doug Gatlin, executive director of Faith and the City in Atlanta, points out that religious faith is marginalized in the great debates taking place in our civic and communal lives. Despite the reality that our legal, economic, and social lives have been shaped by our religious and faith traditions over the centuries, we are increasingly trying to deny the faith traditions that are our civic legacies. Gatlin says, "The notion of separation of church and state is metamorphosing into the separation of faith and values from government and politics." His question is, who will bring the agenda of the "soul of the city to the table?"[1] Indeed, an aggressive secularism, which seeks to remove any acknowledgment of faith traditions from public awareness, seems to be undermining the ability of faith communities to participate in the debates that shape public policy. In fact, if it were left to aggressive secularism, religious faith traditions would be silenced and excluded from public debates altogether.

There are challenges to this contemporary thoroughgoing secularism coming from within academic, theological/religious, and political arenas. Most notable is the challenge from the academic community. This challenge has come from Stephen Carter, an author and professor of law at Yale University School of Law. His concerns are about the artificial separation of church and state and the effort to exclude religion from the public arena. He reminds us that life at its best is a complete, interconnected, and interrelated whole.[2] Separating religious and moral impulses from public life undermines the very essence of the meaning of reality. Moreover, he notes that we are encouraged to act as if our faith does not matter in private or public life and to be ashamed of and keep secret our faith in God.[3]

Influenced by people like Carter, I have become interested in the subject of the overemphasis of the separation of church and state in public debate. More specifically, the pastor as public theologian has been on my mind since President Clinton went through impeachment trials related to his relationship with Monica Lewinsky in 1999. This entire legal process brought to mind the extent to which our culture has gone in making sure that religion is excluded from the public arena.

Former Interdenominational Theological Center (ITC) president Robert Franklin, now Distinguished University Professor at Emory University, introduced the idea of public theologian to ITC in 1997. His thoughts helped me focus on what a public theologian does. For him, a public theologian is one who without apology addresses major public policy concerns and issues from the vantage point of one's faith tradition.[4] With this seminal definition in mind, I wrote an article, cited earlier, addressing President Clinton's problems in response to an invitation to contribute to a publication entitled *Judgment Day at the White House.*[5] My chapter was entitled "African American Pastoral Theology as Public Theology: The Crisis of Private and Public in the White House." In this chapter, I set forth my own understanding of how a pastoral counselor trained in pastoral care and counseling could make a contribution to public concerns raised by President Clinton's problems. I pointed out that my work with people in counseling provided some significant insight into public issues that I felt needed to be part of the public debate about moral, ethical, and boundary issues.

Toward an Understanding of Pastoral Caregiver as Public Theologian

Pastoral counselors have a unique vantage point from which to address public theology. Major issues that take place in wider culture impact our counselees in important ways. For example, Carl Jung, in his publication *Modern Man in Search of Soul*, points out that many dreams of his patients presaged the Second World War.[6] For him, the events in the world and our unconscious selves are intimately connected. Jung's depth psychological perspective need not dominate our discussion, however. Contemporary counselees are influenced in a very conscious way by the dominant conversations that take place in our culture. Counselees continually evaluate what takes place in the lives of significant cultural celebrities, and what they conclude impacts the way they feel about themselves and the way they live their lives. The lives of the rich and famous help to shape the dominant conversations that inform our lives. This is one of the reasons that we are preoccupied with the lives of famous people. The lives of cultural celebrities seem to provide the benchmark conversations for all of us, and all other conversations are influenced by these benchmark conversations.

One method of assessing the interconnection between our private and public lives is to attend to the conversations that inform our behavior. Conversational theory is an approach to public theology that enables us to connect the private and public lives of people as well as the private and public spheres of our life together. The basic assumption in conversational theory is that human beings learn by internalizing the dominant conversations that take place in their lives. Conversational theory is part of narrative psychology, which emphasizes that people learn by internalizing or storying their experiences. Story and conversation are linked in that stories often take the form of conversations in which people participate, and stories form the context for the most significant conversations that inform who we are.

Of critical importance for us here is the conversational theory of Michael White, a noted Australian family therapist. He suggests that human beings, and particularly minorities, are recruited into stories and conversations by wider culture. These stories and conversations are not always congruent with their own identities and experiences.[7] Thus, therapy becomes helping people to edit the stories and conversations that they have internalized that are not always congruent with who they are.

Internalized conversations take on the form of what I call personal mythologies. Personal mythologies are the beliefs and convictions that inform who we are, what we do, and how we interact with others.[8] They tell us how we feel about ourselves, the world we live in, and how we feel about others. Our self-esteem and our outlook on the world are greatly determined by these beliefs and convictions.

In attempting to address these internalized and incongruent conversations, pastoral counselors and psychotherapists often encounter the dominant myths of our culture. These dominant myths often form ideal images of what it means to be human, and these ideal images often reflect images of what it means to be worthwhile in materialistic, popular, and successful terms. Such images often define self-worth in terms of commodities. Human worth is reduced to a commodity that can be bought and sold on the open market. Our worth is defined by our resume rather than by our inherent worth as children of God. In a conception of the self defined exclusively by the market-driven resume, human worth is determined by an honor and shame system of success and failure. All religiously based references to self-worth as a gift from God are not welcomed or understood.

Public theology and pastoral counseling meet in the process of helping people to work through the conversations that inform their self-worth. All persons who are exposed to Western culture for prolonged periods are recruited into the dominant conversations that are market driven and commercial in nature. Other subconversations that ground self-worth and dignity on nonmarketing and noncommodified terms are often marginalized, and the role of the pastoral counselor as public theologian is to help individuals and wider culture to become aware of these alternative human worth conversations. The pastoral counselor and psychotherapist spend time with persons in counseling, helping them to sort through the different conversations and edit them in light of images of one's true worth. The public theologian, drawing on images of human worth from his or her faith tradition, addresses public policy debates and public conversations in light of faith-oriented images of human worth.

In summary, market-driven images of self-worth are often internalized at the expense of other conversations. The role of pastoral counseling and psychotherapy is to help people become aware of how these images of self-worth have impacted their lives and to help them find alternative and more growth-facilitating images of their worth. The public theologian, also drawing on faith perspectives about human worth and experiences in pastoral counseling and psychotherapy, becomes a public critic promoting non-commodity-oriented images of human worth that can provide resources for public policies and planning.

Given the above discussion, the meaning of the pastoral theologian as public theologian can be defined as follows: A pastoral counselor as public theologian offers alternative visions of human worth and value in public discussions that challenge market-driven and commodity-oriented images of self-worth. The counselor's faith orientation and experiences provide the norms and sources for these alternative visions of human worth. Such a view of the public role of the pastoral counselor takes seriously the role of the pastoral counselor as social critic as well as a pastoral caregiver.

Pastoral Caregiving and Public Theology as a Movement

Pastoral theology as cultural critic is a recent movement within the pastoral theological movement that is related specifically to pastoral counseling and care. The Society of Pastoral Theology was formed in 1985 by a group of persons teaching pastoral care and counseling in theological schools and by persons practicing pastoral care and counseling in pastoral counseling centers and doing chaplaincy work in hospitals. The group was formed based on the principle of inclusion grounded in a critique of our racial- and gender-exclusive policies that are part of our cultural heritage in the United States. Thus, from its inception, the Society for Pastoral Theology understood the connection between wider cultural images of human worth and pastoral care and counseling.

The Society of Pastoral Theology took up the topic of public theology in its 1999 annual meeting. Larry Kent Graham and Homer U. Ashby Jr. were the plenary speakers. Graham spoke of the pastoral theologian as cultural critic, and Ashby addressed the concerns of the common good and the separation of church and state. Graham gave good background for understanding our task to define the role of pastoral theologian as public theologian. Some time is spent here focusing on how he defined the task of the pastoral public theologian. In addition to the work of Graham and Ashby, I summarize the overview of the development of pastoral theology given by Bonnie J. Miller-McLemore. I then explore my own effort to address cultural criticism using the theory of modernity and postmodernity.

Larry Kent Graham

Graham outlines the diverse dimensions of pastoral theology as public theology. For him, pastoral public theology is a branch of theology that (1) constructs theories and practices of personal and corporate care; (2) contributes to the common good by identifying, evaluating, and modifying practices, core meaning systems, and normative value systems that impact individuals and groups; and (3) develops norms for the public debate that guide our life together, our practical strategies of sustaining, guiding, and healing, and the liberation of people and the common order.[9] The public pastoral theologian critiques the dominant understandings and practices of culture, including its values, theories of knowing, symbols, and metaphors. Moreover, he or she also provides new options for revision of cultural understandings and practices.[10]

Modernity is the dominant theme that public pastoral theology criticizes, according to Graham. Public theology emerged as a reaction to the pervasive influence of modernity on our understanding of human beings. Modernity is a way of understanding people and reality as a whole, influenced by Cartesian philosophy, a market-driven economy, and the technological and scientific revolutions. Public pastoral theologians bring critical awareness of the impact of modernity on cultural practices and understandings of certain values particularly, that it emphasizes including the split between the private and public spheres, the pushing of religious values and faith to the periphery of society, and the pervasive secularism that helps to define notions of order and freedom which undergird our legal system and Constitution. In Graham's mind, public pastoral theologians agree that our task is to put forward in public debate notions of human nature and institutional growth and development that neither compartmentalize nor reduce life only to mechanistic and economic categories. Thus, the public pastoral theologian joins in public debate, helping to configure the common good and drawing on what Graham calls the micro-systemic window provided by faith and the practice of pastoral counseling.

Graham recognizes that pastoral care and counseling is a child of modernity, and as such it needs to be self-critical as well. He cites its emphasis on individualism, privacy, and subjectivity as examples of the influence of modernity, yet he points out that the movement of pastoral care and counseling has come of age socially through recognizing its social and cultural location and the need to expand its ideas, concepts, and theories. Thus, he points out that pastoral care and counseling has moved from an exclusive orientation on the "living human document" consisting of individuals and their families to a much broader and inclusive notion focused on the "living human web." The notion of the living human web came as a result of the influence of womanist and feminist images of human nature, family therapy, systems family analysis, intercultural and global conversation, and liberation and political theologies.[11]

While Graham is accurate about the shift in pastoral care and counseling away from its individualistic and privatistic notions toward a macro-systemic view, the presence of these inclusive forces historically emerged earlier than Graham indicates. For example, systemic notions of pastoral care can be seen as early as the 1970s in the works of Don Browning, Vincent Foley, Homer Jernigan, Howard Clinebell, Charles Kemp, Archie Smith, and Ed Wimberly. While gender inclusiveness had not emerged as a central issue in the early 1970s, there is evidence that the contextual, systemic, and intercultural awareness was part of the written work of those mentioned above.

Bonnie Miller-McLemore

A full description of the development of pastoral theology as public theology has been done by Bonnie Miller-McLemore.[12] Her historical review is helpful in that it connects pastoral theology as public theology to the discipline of theology. For her, public theology at the University of Chicago helped to shape the development of pastoral theology as public theology, particularly with the students of Don Browning.

The debates between the Chicago school of public theology and the Yale school of public theology is instructive for our discussion. According to Miller-McLemore, the key issue relates to how the faith traditions out of which the theologian came would be entered into public debates around crucial issues impacting the public good. The concern is whether Christianity's distinctiveness gets compromised in public debates or whether one entered the debate with the unique language and rules of Christianity.[13] Whether one adhered to the Chicago school or the Yale school, the key concern was that theology and pastoral theology had to be part of the public debates if they were to remain faithful to Christianity.

Miller-McLemore also points out that liberation theology brought a new dimension to the public debates by focusing on the marginalized and silent voices. Liberation theology wanted to make sure that the powerful voices were not the only voices heard in public debates. More than this, she points out that the personal is political, and that powerful social forces in society shape the self.[14]

While the notions of pastoral theologian as public theologian are new and relate to the latter part of the 1990s, I laid some of the groundwork for a public theological view in my 1975 doctoral dissertation and later in a publication in 1982 entitled *Pastoral Counseling and Spiritual Values: A Black Point of View*. The purpose of such a review is to show continuity with the present movement in pastoral public theology with the development of African American pastoral care and counseling.

African American Pastoral Caregiving as Public Pastoral Theology

As early as 1970, there was awareness that the traditional one-to-one model of psychology did not address the multidimensional problems that faced the African American community.[15] In the 1970s liberation of African Americans from social oppression was the dominant agenda, and psychological approaches to solving human problems did not seem relevant. Only the psychology that addressed human problems within a social context was given a hearing. Moreover, psychology that addressed the connection between racism and psychological pathology would be considered to be relevant.

Because of the peculiar needs of African Americans in the racial climate of the United States, the conceptualization of African American pastoral care began as a critique of modernity, and its conceptual theories were akin to the themes in public theology. For example, several important themes were addressed in the early stages of African American pastoral care. The first theme had to do with the total dimensions of the human personality and its corporate nature as opposed to a strictly intra-psychic orientation.[16] Social forces such as inequality, injustice, and racism necessitated a personality theory that was contextual in nature.

Another theme was the protest nature of ministry in the black community resulting from the civil rights movement of the 1950s and 1960s. To be consistent with the protest tradition related to ministry, African American pastoral care had to include social and political action. Thus, at the beginning stages of African American pastoral care there was a major concern for making the public aware of the impact of racism on the lives of African Americans.

A third theme dealt with the role of the local black congregation as a support system and refuge to address the many needs of African Americans. The role of the local black congregation in being a cathartic center for healing damaged emotions, for providing rituals and belief systems for handling negative personal and social experiences, and for providing resources for fostering self-esteem and identity validation were all originating ideas of African American pastoral care.

A final theme in the origin of conceptual pastoral care in the black church was the awareness of how God worked in history and in the lives of the black community. The ideas of separating church and state or faith and life were not part of the African American worldview.

These four themes — the holistic nature of personality, the protest theme, the corporate nature of the local congregation as a support system, and a view of God as one who is intimately involved in the lives of the community and the lives of people — all reflect a postmodern trend. The postmodern trend is characterized by (1) approaches that defy individualism, (2) ideas and methods that see the interrelationship between social forces and the growth of persons, and (3) ideas and methods that refuse to separate faith and life. Moreover, African American conceptual pastoral care understands that theories of personalities must be based on contextual psychological models and intervention models that address social problems along with individual problems. Additionally, the protest theme was a forerunner to the public theological model, because social protest was a means of making public certain problems that public policy needed to address. African American pastoral care is a significant development in the history of pastoral care in the United States, and it began as a counter-modernizing trend.

In the 1982 publication *Pastoral Counseling and Spiritual Values: A Black Point of View*, I set out systematically to address the theme of modernity.[17] The motivation for writing this present book stems from the awareness that the forces of modernity are undermining the institutional support structures of the black church in the African American experience. Therefore, I try here to lay a critical theoretical foundation for addressing the negative impact of modernity on the black church as an institution. Consequently, this originating concern for the impact of modernity on individuals and institutions was similar to the motivation that later gave rise to the public theology movement in the 1990s.

Contemporary public theology provides a critique of modernity as well as alternative theories that need to be part of public debates. The critical thrusts of public theology as well as alternative theories challenging the prevailing models of modernity can be gleaned from African American pastoral care. For example, modernity was defined as "... transformation socially, politically, psychologically, and religiously, brought about by technology and reflecting the uprooting of beliefs and values from modern life."[18] This understanding of modernity also reflected other important themes treated in sociology, namely, privatism and secularism. Part of modernity is a form of individualism in which individuals select their own values from a large pool of competing values, which is viewed as problematic when secularism emphasizes that religious references to values need to be excluded from discussions of values.[19] The threat is that privatism accompanied by secular influences could separate faith and values from public life.

This threat of modernity to the black church was viewed as real. For example, the following quotation is instructive regarding the impact of modernity on the role of the black church:

> Many of the support structures and traditions of the black church, which have been conveyers and custodians of past cherished values, are now feeling the slicing cut of the sharp blades of modern progress. We are stumbling into an era when traditional values will have less impact upon our lives as individuals, even when we remain vigilant to preserve these values.[20]

In short, it is essential to attend quite intentionally to preserving the support system functions of local black congregations.

In that book the concept of a mediating structure was used to conceptualize the intentional nature of the task. Mediating structures are those institutions that stand between the individual and wider society or between the private and public spheres of life. These institutions are the family, extended family, neighborhood, the village, the church, and a whole host of voluntary groups where there are continual face-to-face relationships.[21]

Models for preserving the local black congregation in the face of modernity come from behavioral and social sciences that are contextual. They include developmental and growth psychologies, family systems theory, organizational systems theories, network theories, community organization theories, preventive psychological approaches, public health approaches, and many others.

This brief review sets the stage for a contemporary approach to pastoral theology as public theology. The next section describes a new threat that has emerged for the black church: the nihilism that is one result of modernity, and which is actively undermining black churches. African American pastoral care in the twenty-first century must take this new threat seriously.

African American Public Pastoral Theology and Nihilism

Perhaps the most devastating impact of modernity is the creation of relational refugees. Relational refugees are those who have been recruited by the wider culture to think that being cut off from relationships is the source of growth and life enhancement. More precisely, relational refugees are those who seek to actualize the major market-driven values of our society by allowing themselves to be cut off from their family and communal roots.[22]

> Peter Berger and his colleagues discuss the types of persons I am interested in as those who suffer from a homeless mind. Berger is interested in the ways people use images from social and economic life to shape their self-identity. One such image equates self with a machine. This image compartmentalizes life into private and public spheres, detaching self from feelings. People whose dominant self-image is that of a computer construct virtual worlds. These worlds encourage withdrawal from, rather than engagement in, nurturing relationships. To live as a computer is to live as a refugee.[23]

Indeed, the relational refugee has been recruited into a conversation that disengages him or her from his or her relational roots, yet our need to be significantly related to others throughout our life cycle does not disappear. Rather, our relational needs become subconscious, and we began to seek substitutes for relationships through different forms of addiction, including addictions to substances, food, and sex. Modern addictions are fantasized ways of coping with our basic need for love and community.

Pastoral counseling becomes the arena where relational refugees end up when they have to begun to edit the conversations and personal myths built on personal isolation. The work of the pastoral counselor is to be a relational presence for the relational refugee so that he or she has constant companionship when re-editing or re-authoring those conversations into which they have been recruited.

The relational refugee is very vulnerable. Being detached and isolated makes one a victim of his or her inner psychological life, as well as to the physical, mental, and spiritual problems of being detached. In our Western culture, the major danger is addictions of many kinds as well as early death. Because of the basic danger and vulnerability that the relational refugee faces, it is urgent that the pastoral theologian becomes a cultural critic, lifting up images of what it means to be fully human throughout the life cycle, meaning primarily to be in relationships.

In summary, this chapter has outlined the role of pastoral caregivers as public theologians. Crucial roles include being a cultural critic and joining the public debate by offering alternative conversations based on a theological anthropology rooted in faith and in the behavioral and social sciences.

The chapter also emphasized that it is not enough to liberate personal agency in counselees. Attention must be given to the way society attempts to recruit people into stories, plots, ideas, and images that are alien to who they are. For that reason, critiquing modernity and introducing themes of wholeness of persons into public debate are important dimensions of public theology.

Chapter Seven

The Formation of a
Public Pastoral Theologian

T HIS CHAPTER suggests how to bring about the formation
of public practical theologians, those who can provide leadership not only within congregations and religious
institutions but also in the public and political arena.

Framing the Problem

A public theologian is one who is able to enter public policy debates addressing issues and concerns of the day from
the point of view of one's faith tradition.[1] Whether religious
leaders perceive themselves as prophets, priests, or apostles, a
central value in many faith traditions is that religious leaders need to take seriously their role as public theologians.
In our Cartesian age of breaking life up into discrete enti-
ties, we often want to make different approaches to ministry
distinct and mutually exclusive. Yet, in our postmodern men-
tality, we are recognizing that our roles, tasks, and approaches
to ministry are in fact interconnected. Moreover, the institutions that support our ministries are holistic and organic in
nature, and therefore should never be conceived of as unrelated constituent parts. Consequently, we all have a role to
play in being public theologians, whether prophet, priest, or

apostle. We should not separate the life within our religious institutions from the life of the world. Public life and private life are never mutually exclusive, but rather intimately connected.

In contemporary theological education, different dimensions or approaches to ministry are held in mutual tension. Seminaries are to prepare leadership for the different dimensions and approaches to ministry within church and the world. Leadership is fundamental to what religious functionaries are to do. Leadership is a complex concept, but it generally refers to having a vision of what needs to be accomplished in a particular setting and helping people move in the direction of that vision.

There was a time in theological education when prophetic leadership was more valued than other aspects of leadership. For example, during the civil rights struggles of the 1950s and 1960s many seminaries emphasized the prophetic role of leadership, particularly to use the resources of the church to promote justice and liberation of oppressed people. The role of priests was to carry out the worship and liturgical tasks within congregations, and apostles performed the caregiving and nurturing functions in order to develop persons and congregations. During the time when the prophetic role was prominent, the priestly and apostolic dimensions were both secondary. Today, however, ministry is understood to be much more inclusive and interrelated. Regardless of our personal ministry style preferences, today we are viewed, more than was the case in the past, as having a public role to play.

Theological education has, indeed, matured to the level of being interdisciplinary and multifaceted. The key emphasis today is on carrying out the task of theological training by emphasizing the public dimension of leadership, no matter which of the three roles one prefers. We all have a role in participating in shaping public policy, according to contemporary ministry wisdom.

Given this emphasis on holistic ministry, seminaries need to prepare pastors to be ready to provide leadership on public issues. For example, public policies impact local congregations all the time, and local pastors and their congregations must enter public debate continually to carry out their ministry. Megachurches are running into zoning restrictions and neighborhood opposition to their expansion. The government's use of faith-based organizations to carry out services beneficial to the entire community requires a level of civic sophistication to access public funding. Knowing how to access the political process is also essential for religious leaders. Theological education must prepare its students for leadership both within religious institutions as well as in the public arena.

Formation of theological students who can provide leadership in religious institutions and who can enter the public policy debates with facility and ability is a fundamental concern. Theological education has not always been comfortable with formation concerns, particularly because formation evokes notions of indoctrination, lack of academic freedom, and growth-blocking in the minds of faculty. Yet seminaries are now being forced to address formation issues because of the leadership problems facing seminary students upon graduation. Moreover, secular accrediting bodies are insisting that seminary student outcome measurements be consistent with what seminaries say in their mission and goal statements; therefore, seminaries are having to attend to specific religious and secular concerns that necessitate attention to formation issues more than was the case in the past.

Theological Formation at ITC

Many conversations take place in theological education, and students need to select from a great variety what will be meaningful for them for their learning. While what each student internalizes from the curriculum is unique, there are crucial commitments of faculty members of the place I teach, the Interdenominational Theological Center in Atlanta, that inform the conversational environment undergirding what we do in formation, just as there are in other places where people teach or minister. One such commitment is to critical reasoning, particularly where students are able to assess the experiences they bring to seminary by drawing on a variety of perspectives in their assessment. Another commitment is the belief that a major tool of ministry is the personhood of the student. Third, there is a commitment to making sure students embrace the need for them to address public issues that impact people's lives. Our faculty as a whole recognizes a vital connection between all three commitments mentioned above. Students' ability to be public theologians who address public issues is enhanced by helping them develop their ability to critically assess their experiences as well as enable them to grow in their personal lives.

One of our students came to ITC from a political career as an elected official in city government in a southwestern city.[2] She points out that her experience as a student involved in the curriculum of ITC was very exciting, because she experienced a great deal of coherence and consistency among the different courses she was taking. For example, many of the courses appeared to carry a similar expectation that she bring her own experiences in life into dialogue with what was being learned in class. Thus, courses in the Hebrew Bible and in the New Testament taught her to think critically about what she learned about the Bible from the original shaping communities of her childhood and youth. Growing up, she learned a lot about the role and place of women in the Bible. Some things were positive and some things were negative, but her courses in Bible at ITC helped her to discern more possibilities for the role of women biblically than she had brought with her to seminary. In addition, she found that what her Sunday school teacher had taught her about seeing herself in the stories of scripture was supported by what she was learning in her classes. In short, she learned that reader-focused interpretation of the Bible deriving from inserting oneself into the stories of scripture was legitimate.

Another significant aspect of the curriculum was having her assumptions about people challenged in class. She came to seminary with a great deal of experience in social work and in leadership as an elected official and as an employee. She indicated that she learned some things in her field placement in seminary that caused her to reevaluate some assumptions she had previously made about people, particularly about those people who struggled with and were often defeated by crack cocaine. She said that seminary taught her to rethink and reevaluate prejudices she had built up over time, and it taught her not to view people in categories that prevented her from seeing growth possibilities in them. Seminary also encouraged her to engage people through entering their stories and journeying along with them by actively listening to them.

She gave a vivid example of one woman who was recovering from drug addiction. She encountered this woman who had been addicted to crack cocaine for fifteen years. Before giving into crack cocaine, however, this woman was successful. She had a family, had secured a nice house and car, and was well respected in the community. Despite her success, she had such a deep fear of failing that she attempted to find an escape from her fear of success, first by turning to cocaine offered to her by a relative at a social occasion. Later, she switched from powder cocaine to crack because it was cheaper. As a result, she became addicted. Because of her addiction, she had been imprisoned, worked the streets as a prostitute, and had been institutionalized as mentally ill.

Connie met this woman in her field placement as part of her seminary experience at one of the community centers. Connie indicated that something dramatic happened when she was in conversation with this woman, when the woman turned the tables on her and began to focus on Connie. The conversation went like this:

"Rev. Jackson, may I ask you a few questions?" I said, "Sure, fire away." She asked, "Did your Mom and Dad take you to Sunday school, and not just send you, but did they physically go with you?" I said, "Yes." The woman said, "I used to be you." She then asked: "Before you came to ITC to study theology, did you have a good-paying job?" I said, "I did." She said, "I used to be you." She continued: "You are an articulate sister. I bet you are pretty smart and do well academically, am I right?" I said, "I made good grades here and there." She said, "I used to be you." She then asked, "Do you have dreams of being a great person and helping lots of people one day?" I replied, "Of course." She said, "I used to be you." It was at that moment I realized the stark message she was sending to me. If she used to me some years ago, then Connie Jackson could very well be her today.

Connie then went on to describe how her seminary courses helped her to assess herself and her work. She said seminary helped her to assess what she brought to seminary. She encountered this woman through a missiology course assignment, and learned to listen to her story and take it seriously through what she had learned in a class about liberation theology. These two courses highlight how the theological curriculum works in an interdisciplinary way to form students. Connie said she had never before heard or seen so many different stories of people who did not make good on their promises to turn their lives around. As a result she said she had become desensitized to really listening to more stories and was likely to believe that people were not really serious about deliverance or rehabilitation. By entering this woman's life through story, however, she became less cynical and renewed her commitment to begin listening again. She was able to visualize this woman anew, beyond the stereotypes of female drug addicts she had internalized in her earlier work experiences. She said liberation theology helped her to see that God was present and at work in the lives of people, regardless of the dire circumstances in which people found themselves.

She also indicated that her biblical courses not only helped her to relate her own experiences to Bible situations, but they also helped her relate the woman's story to stories in the Bible. She said, "Exposure to the kind of biblical studies curriculum that teaches you to contemporize the biblical text and make it applicable to today is what made the difference in my attitude toward the woman that day."

She went on to talk about courses that forced her to leave the seminary campus and go out into the community. This was essential for her learning, and it made a big difference to her. She was forced to interact with people who were different from her and other seminarians. She found out, however, that this woman's earlier life was not that different from her own. They both had similar backgrounds, but certain circumstances and choices this woman made undermined her life.

Connie gave high marks to the different professors at ITC with whom she has had classes. She found that many professors realized the significance of helping students to assess their life experiences from different perspectives. They wanted her to discover her own voice as she progressed through the curriculum so that what she appropriated was truly her own understanding, her own theology. Moreover, they provided learning situations where she was able to link what she was learning in the classroom to what was going on in the community. She concludes that she was able to envisage ministry in ways that link what was going on in the church to public issues and concerns. In short, seminary deepened her formation as a minister who was a public theologian. She found seminary helpful in providing an environment of discourse, conversation, and experiences that broadened her understanding of ministry and facilitated her personal growth.

Connie was not convinced that all students respond to theological education in the way that she did; not all of them want to fully engage the process in the way she did. She would like her seminary to be more intentional in encouraging students in engaging theological education in ways that transform students' lives.

Conversation and Formation

There are persons who make a contribution to understanding the role of formation in the theological educational process. Many historians, philosophers, and practitioners from a variety of disciplines and professions understand formation in theological education. I have found the work of Garth Kasimu Baker-Fletcher essential in understanding the place of discourse and conversation in the theological education formation process. He talks about the function of critical theory in ethical and moral reflection.[3] Baker-Fletcher draws on the thinking of Jürgen Habermas, Michel Foucault, and Pierre Bourdieu to expound on the role of conversation and discourse in the development of moral reasoning.

For Baker-Fletcher, "Critical theory attempts to unearth the historical and social genesis of the facts it examines and the social contexts in which its results will have their effects."[4] He points out that practices and conversations have their own historical contexts. The purpose of moral reasoning and critical thinking is to place practices and conversations into big pictures and grand narratives, so that they can be constructed, deconstructed, and reconstructed. This was what Connie Jackson was doing. The conversation about her educational environment helped to internalize the need to put her life and her experiences with others into broader perspectives and into grander narratives. As a result, she was able to assess what was helpful and not so helpful in what she brought to seminary and to ministry. Learning to allow others to tell their stories and to see how these stories fit into what God was doing helped her to develop critical reasoning. She learned to let go of her preconceived ideas about certain people who struggled with substance addiction. In other words, she developed critical and analytic thinking.

Baker-Fletcher's thought has implications for formation in theological education. First, individuals bring with them to theological education an orientation to moral reasoning. Second, this orientation has a social context influenced by conversations or discourses that they have heard over the years. Third, there are conversations in theological education to which the student will be exposed, which have the potential of altering the orientation to moral reasoning that the student brings to seminary. Fourth, conversations within the professional environment reflect conversations taking place in wider culture. Fifth, these conversations often reflect the negative attitudes some people have — in this case, toward those who suffer from substance abuse.

Connie's experience at seminary reflected all these dimensions and more. Her personal growth was affected by the seminary experience where she learned the connection between her own growth and empathy toward others. As she learned more about herself, she also learned to listen to others. For her, there was a correlation between self-awareness and the needs of others. Thus, as she grew in her faith, she also saw God at work in the lives of others. She was able to discern God at work in others when she was able to see God at work in herself.

Formation and Authentic Living

In the case of Connie Jackson we get a glimpse of how her personal growth contributed to her social awareness of the needs of others. Throughout this book I have tried to show a connection between such development of personal agency and awareness and the manifestation of political efficacy. Connie's formation in theological education increased her personal voice and growth, and she was able to turn this growth and agency into service to others and to the public arena.

This book has highlighted the key role of personal agency and how it leads to political efficacy particularly within African American religious settings. In fact, the transition from personal agency to political efficacy must be seen within the social worldview of African American religious people, and the same might not hold true for non–African American religion, given its individualistic orientation. Formation that takes seriously personal agency must also take into account the formational context particularly within the local African American congregation, which typically links personal agency to political efficacy, service, and vocation. The connection between personal agency and political efficacy is not necessarily automatic.

Consequently, formation in African American theological education must take seriously the practices of self outlined in this manuscript. In chapter 4, I talked about the practices of self leading to authentic living. Authentic living calls for congruence between one's private life and one's public life. Such authentic living involves practices of re-storying, returning to unfinished family business, increased self-awareness, moving toward transparency, editing conversations into which one has been recruited, and other practices. Seminary education provides opportunities and a safe environment for this to happen. Furthermore, the practices of self also include self-awareness as a process of recognizing how wider social contextual conversations impact one's development. In this context, chapter 5 explored how modernity helps to reduce our self-worth to a commodity and how such a view undermines our worth and value. Moreover, the practices of self also include making our relationship and conversation with God primary so that formation becomes spiritual formation. In other words, formation in theological education is a holistic process involving all aspects of the curriculum as well as processes explicated in this chapter.

The formation process in theological education therefore involves several key elements. First, the formation of public pastoral theologians must be holistic. Second, holism involves sorting through cultural conversations in a critical way. Third, we must be attentive to God's role in this process. Fourth, seminaries must provide opportunities for critical engagement in teaching and in conversations so that students develop tools of critical self- and social awareness. Fifth, theological students are called to learn to think critically about what they bring to seminary and welcome the shaping that the educational and formational processes of theological education bring to their experiences and beliefs. Sixth and finally, the formation process needs to help students become public pastoral theologians by enabling them to engage the formation process in a way that critically challenges the conversation that separates faith from public debate, the spiritual from the secular, and the private from the public. An integrated conversation has the possibility of moving people from oppression to empowerment, the best of political change.

Notes

Foreword

1. Martin Luther King Jr., *Where Do We Go from Here: Chaos or Community?* (New York: Harper & Row, 1967), 211.

Preface

1. Robert M. Franklin indicates that the quest of African Americans has been to participate fully in wider society. See *Another Day's Journey: Black Churches Confronting the American Crisis* (Minneapolis: Fortress Press, 1997), 2.

2. Lee G. Bolman and Terrence E. Deal, *Reframing Organizations: Artistry, Choice, and Leadership* (San Francisco: Jossey-Bass, 2003), 186–87.

3. Bonnie J. Miller-McLemore, "Pastoral Theology as Public Theology: Revolutions in the 'Fourth Area,'" in *Pastoral Care and Counseling: Redefining the Paradigms*, ed. Nancy J. Ramsay (Nashville: Abingdon Press, 2004), 45–64.

Chapter 1: African American Pastoral Care and Counseling as Political Processes

1. Homer U. Ashby Jr., *Our Home Is over Jordan* (St. Louis: Chalice Press, 2003).

2. Ibid., 1–15.

3. Ibid., 6.

4. Ibid., 12.

5. Michel Foucault, *The Archaeology of Knowledge and the Discourse on Language* (New York: Pantheon Books, 1972), 46.

6. Ibid., 51.

7. See James Perryman, *Unfounded Loyalty: An In-Depth Look into the Love Affair between Blacks and Democrats* (Lanham, MD: Pneuma Life Publishing, 2003).

8. See Edward P. Wimberly, *Claiming God, Reclaiming Dignity: African American Pastoral Care* (Nashville: Abingdon Press, 2003).

9. Margaret Patricia Aymer, "First Pure, Then Peaceable: Frederick Douglass Reads James," PhD dissertation, Union Theological Seminary, New York, 2004.

10. Walter Earl Fluker, "Recognition, Respectability, and Loyalty: Black Churches and the Quest for Civility," in *New Day Begun: African American Churches and Civic Culture in Post–Civil Rights America*, ed. R. Drew Smith (Durham, NC: Duke University Press, 2003), 113–41.

11. Fredrick C. Harris, *Something Within: Religion in African-American Activism* (New York: Oxford University Press, 1999), 81–85.

12. Ibid.

13. See Edward P. Wimberly, *Pastoral Counseling and Spiritual Values* (Nashville: Abingdon Press, 1982). See also Edward P. Wimberly, *Relational Refugee* (Nashville: Abingdon Press, 2000).

14. Michel Foucault, *The Care of the Self: The History of Sexuality* (New York: Vintage Books, 1988), 81–95.

15. Emmanuel Y. Lartey, *In Living Colour: An Intercultural Approach to Pastoral Care and Counseling* (London: Cassell, 1997).

16. Ibid., 79–81.

17. Ibid., 94–102.

18. Ibid.

19. Cornel West, *Race Matters* (New York: Vintage Books, 1994), 17–31.

20. Ibid., 20.

21. Archie Smith Jr., *The Relational Self: Ethics and Therapy from a Black Church Perspective* (Nashville: Abingdon Press, 1982).

22. Ibid., 62–64.

23. Ibid., 71–72.

24. Carroll A. Watkins Ali, *Survival and Liberation: Pastoral Theology in African American Context* (St. Louis: Chalice Press, 1999), 2.

25. A. Elaine Crawford, *Hope in the Holler: A Womanist Theology* (Louisville: Westminster John Knox, 2002), xvi.

26. Plenary presentation at the Society for Pastoral Theology annual meeting in Atlanta, June 2004.

27. Ashby, *Our Home Is over Jordan*, 37–42.

28. Ibid., 39.

Chapter 2: The Parish Context of African American Pastoral Counseling

1. Michel Foucault, *The Birth of the Clinic: An Archaeology of Medical Perception* (New York: Vintage Books, 1973), xv–xix.

2. Michael White provides this understanding of remembering practices in *Narratives of Therapists' Lives* (Adelaide, South Australia: Dulwich Centre Publications, 1997), 8.

3. Edward P. Wimberly, *Recalling Our Own Stories: Spiritual Renewal for Religious Caregivers* (San Francisco: Jossey-Bass, 1997).

4. White, *Narratives of Therapists' Lives*, 22.

5. See Norman Cameron, *Personality Development and Psychopathology: A Dynamic Approach* (Boston: Houghton Mifflin, 1963), 650–51.

6. See Catherine Owens Peare, *Mary McLead Bethune* (New York: Vanguard Press, 1951) for stories of how the prohibition against African Americans reading survived slavery.

7. C. G. Jung, *Psychology and Education* (Princeton, NJ: Bollinger Series, Princeton University Press, 1954). This book was the result of translating four of eight essays in vol. 17 of the *Collected Works*. Three of the essays were published in *Psychologie und Erziehung* (1946).

8. Ibid., 129–30.

9. Ibid.

10. Ibid., 130.

11. Christine Y. Wiley, "The Impact of a Parish-Based Pastoral Counseling Center on Counselors and Congregation: A Womanist Perspective," DMin dissertation, Garrett-Evangelical Theological Seminary, Evanston, IL, 1994.

12. Don S. Browning, *A Fundamental Practical Theology: Descriptive and Strategic Proposals* (Minneapolis: Fortress Press, 1991), 243–77.

13. Ibid., 253.

14. Ibid., 256.

15. Ibid.

16. Ibid., 253.

Chapter 3: Liberation from Oppressive Conversations

1. E. Lynn Harris, *What Becomes of the Brokenhearted* (New York: Doubleday, 2003).

2. Ibid., xi.

3. Ibid.

4. Ibid., 2.

5. Ibid., 19.

6. This insight has come from a study authorized by the Carnegie Foundation for the Advancement of Teaching, entitled *Educating Clergy*, by Charles R. Foster, Lisa Dahill, Larry Golemon, and Barbara Tolentino. The insights are built on the work of William Lebeau, "Rabbinic Education for the 21st Century," *Sh'ma: A Journal of Jewish Responsibility* 527 (1997); *www.shma.com/jan03/Lebeau.htm*.

7. Harris, *What Becomes of the Brokenhearted*, 229.

8. E. Lynn Harris, *Abide with Me* (New York: Anchor Books, 2000), 349–50.

9. Ellen Charry, *By the Renewing of Your Mind: The Pastoral Function of Christian Doctrine* (New York: Oxford University Press, 1997).

10. Harris, *What Becomes of the Brokenhearted*, 215.

11. Ibid.

12. Ibid., 220, 235, and 246.

13. Ibid., 192.

14. Linda H. Hollies, *Inner Healing for Broken Vessels: Seven Steps to Mending Childhood Wounds* (New York: Welstar Publications, 1990), 68; reissued as *Inner Healing for Broken Vessels: A Domestic Violence Survival Guide* (Cleveland: Pilgrim Press, 2006).

15. Ibid., 68–69.

16. A. Elaine Brown Crawford, *Hope in the Holler: A Womanist Theology* (Louisville: Westminster John Knox, 2002), xvi.

17. Hollies, *Inner Healing for Broken Vessels*, xii.

18. Ibid.

19. Ibid., 68–69.

20. Wilson Goode, *In Goode Faith* (Valley Forge, PA: Judson Press, 1992), 32.

21. Ibid., xii.

22. Ibid., 47.

23. Ibid., 65.

24. Henry H. Mitchell and Nicolas Cooper Lewter, *Soul Theology: The Heart of Black Culture* (San Francisco: Harper and Row, 1986), 14.

25. Charles Gerkin, *Crisis Experience in Modern Life* (Nashville: Abingdon Press, 1979).

26. Charry, *By the Renewing of Your Mind*, 133.

Chapter 4: Practicing Authentic Self-Awareness as Public Theologians

1. For a discussion of the relationship of politics and the role of faith, see Ismael Garcia, "Politics and Religion," *Insights: The Faculty Journal of Austin Seminary* (Fall 2004): 3–12.

2. Ernest J. Gaines, *In My Father's House* (New York: Vintage Books, 1978), 69.

3. E. Hammond Oglesby, *Ethical Issues That Matter: A New Method of Moral Discourse in Church Life* (Lanham, MD: University Press of America, 2002), 2.

4. Ibid., 6.

5. Ibid., 35.

6. Garth Kasimu Baker-Fletcher, *Dirty Hands: Christian Ethics in a Morally Ambiguous World* (Minneapolis: Fortress Press, 2000), 3.

7. Daniel Goleman et al., *Primal Leadership: Learning to Lead with Emotional Intelligence* (Cambridge, MA: Harvard Business School Press, 2002), 39.

8. Ibid.

9. Ibid.

10. Ibid.

11. Ibid.

12. Ibid., 33.

13. Gabriel Fackre, "Christian Doctrine and Presidential Decisions," in *Judgment Day at the White House: A Critical Declaration Exploring Moral Issues and the Political Use and Misuse of Religion*, ed. Gabriel J. Fackre (Grand Rapids: Eerdmans, 1999), 103.

14. Edward P. Wimberly, "African-American Pastoral Theology as Public Theology: The Crisis of Private and Public in the White House," in Fackre, *Judgment Day in the White House*, 90.

15. Ibid., 92.

16. *60 Minutes* interview with Dan Rather, June 20, 2004.

17. The theme of blind triumphalism relates to a view of suffering growing out of the experiences of the house church in Rome reflected in the book of Romans. Paul was dealing with a more realistic view of suffering because many of the people felt that they would not have to suffer because of the return of Christ. See Robert Jewett, *Romans: Cokesbury Bible Commentary* (Nashville: Graded Press, 1988), 98–99.

18. See Ellen Charry, *By the Renewing of Your Mind: The Pastoral Function of Christian Doctrine* (New York: Oxford University Press, 1997), 133.

19. Ibid., 132.

20. Edward P. Wimberly, *Claiming God, Reclaiming Dignity: African American Pastoral Care* (Nashville: Abingdon Press, 2003). 18.

21. Ibid., 101.

22. Ibid., 99.

Chapter 5: Pastoral Counseling and Critique of Modernity

1. Stephen L. Carter, *The Emperor of Ocean Park* (New York: Alfred A. Knopf, 2002).

2. Ibid., 620.

3. Ibid., 653.

4. Walter Fluker, "Recognition, Respectability, and Loyalty: Black Churches and the Quest for Civility," in *New Day Begun: African American Churches and Civic Culture in Post–Civil Rights America* (Durham, NC: Duke University Press, 2003), 113–41.

5. Cornel West, *Democracy Matters: Winning the Fight against Imperialism* (New York: Penguin Press, 2004), 28–29.

6. Carrie Doehring, in *Taking Care: Monitoring Power Dynamics and Relational Boundaries in Pastoral Care and Counseling* (Nashville: Abingdon Press, 1995).

7. Stephen L. Carter, *Culture of Disbelief: How American Law and Politics Trivialize Religious Devotion* (New York: Doubleday Anchor Books, 1993).

8. Ibid., xiv–xv.

9. Ibid., xvii.

10. Ibid., 14–15.

11. Henry Mitchell and Nicholas Lewter, *Soul Theology: The Heart of Black Culture* (San Francisco: Harper and Row, 1986).

12. Daniel J. Levinson, *Seasons of a Man's Life* (New York: Ballantine Books, 1978).

Chapter 6: Challenging Modernity

1. Doug Gatlin, Charles V. Gerkin Pastoral Care Symposium, October 21, 2002, Norcross, Georgia.

2. Stephen Carter, *Integrity* (New York: Basic Books, 1996), 7–8.

3. Stephen Carter, *The Culture of Disbelief: How American Law and Politics Trivialize Religious Devotion* (New York: Doubleday Anchor Books, 1993), 3–4.

4. Robert Franklin, "Travlin Shoes: Resources for Our Journey," *Journal of the Interdenominational Theological Center* (Fall 1997): 3; *Another Day's Journey: Black Churches Confronting the American Crisis* (Minneapolis: Fortress Press, 1997).

5. Gabriel Fackre, ed., *Judgment Day at the White House: A Critical Declaration Exploring Moral Issues and the Political Use and Abuse of Religion* (Grand Rapids: William B. Eerdmans Publishing, 1999).

6. Carl Jung, *Modern Man in Search of Soul* (New York: Harcourt Brace Jovanovich, 1933).

7. These ideas are based on the following works of Michael White, *Narrative of Therapist's Lives* (Adelaide, South Australia: Dulwich, 1997), and *Re-Authoring Lives: Interviews and Essays* (Adelaide, South Australia: Dulwich, 1995).

8. Edward P. Wimberly, *Recalling Our Own Stories: The Spiritual Care of Religious Caregivers* (San Francisco: Jossey-Bass, 1999).

9. Larry Kent Graham, "Pastoral Theology as Public Theology in Relation to the Clinic," *Journal of Pastoral Theology* 9 (2000): 1–17.

10. Ibid.

11. For discussion of the living human web, see Bonnie J. Miller-McLemore, "Pastoral Theology as Public Theology: Revolutions in the Fourth Area," in *Pastoral Care and Counseling: Redefining the Paradigms,* ed. Nancy Ramsey (Nashville: Abingdon Press, 2004), 45–64.

12. Ibid.

13. Ibid., 48–49.

14. Ibid., 50–51.

15. Edward P. Wimberly, "A Conceptual Model for Pastoral Care in the Black Church Utilizing Systems and Crisis Theories," Boston University Graduate School, 1976, 2.

16. Ibid., 34–39.

17. Edward P. Wimberly, *Pastoral Counseling and Spiritual Values: A Black Point of View* (Nashville: Abingdon Press, 1982).

18. Ibid., 9.

19. Ibid.

20. Ibid.

21. Ibid., 14.

22. Edward P. Wimberly, *Relational Refugee: Alienation and Reincorporation in African American Churches and Communities* (Nashville: Abingdon Press, 2000), 22.

23. Ibid.

Chapter 7: The Formation of a Public Pastoral Theologian

1. Robert Franklin, "Travlin Shoes: Resources for Our Journey," *Journal of the Interdenominational Theological Center* (Fall 1997): 3.

2. Connie Jackson is a senior at ITC and has given me permission to use an assessment assignment she wrote in the Spring semester of 2003. She also provided me with an update via telephone of what she wrote at that time.

3. Garth Kasimu Baker-Fletcher, *Dirty Hands: Christian Ethics in a Morally Ambiguous World* (Minneapolis: Fortress Press, 2000), 53–58.

4. Ibid., 54.